KAFFE FASSETT'S brilliant little patchworks

KAFFE FASSETT'S brilliant little patchworks

PROJECT CONSTRUCTION BY
Margaret Rowan

PHOTOGRAPHY BY
Debbie Patterson

20 stitched and patched projects using Kaffe Fassett fabrics

ROWAN

Brilliant Little Patchworks
First published in the UK in 2015
Rowan
Coats Crafts UK
Green Lane Mill
Holmfirth
HD9 2DX

Created and produced by Berry & Co (Publishing) Ltd
47 Crewys Road
Childs Hill
London NW2 2AU

Copyright © Berry & Co Publishing Ltd 2015
Project designs copyright © Kaffe Fassett 2015

The patchwork designs in this book are copyright and must not be produced for resale.

All rights reserved. No part of this publication may be reproduced, stored in a retrieval system or transmitted in any form or by any means, electronic, electrostatic, magnetic tape, mechanical, photocopying, recording or otherwise, without the prior permission in writing from the copyright holders.

Designer: Anne Wilson
Editor: Katie Hardwicke
Technical editor: Katy Denny
Location photography: Debbie Patterson
Styling: Kaffe Fassett
Project making/instructions: Margaret Rowan
Step photography: Margaret Rowan
Stills photography: Steven Wooster
Illustrations: Therese Chynoweth

British Library Cataloguing and Publication Data
A catalogue record of this book is available from the British Library

ISBN 978-0-9927968-0-8

Reproduced in the UK
Printed in China

Measurement conversions
Please note, the patchwork designs were originally created using imperial measurements. The metric conversions are not direct calculations. Please work in one measurement system, not a mix of the two, to achieve successful results.

Contents

Inspiration and ideas 6

Leafy apron 8
Hexagon bolster 14
Stripes cushions 20
Summer flowers tablecloth 27
Brassica table runner 32
Flower power kimono 36
Big blooms miniquilt 42
Fiesta floor cushion 48
Blues table runner and mats 56
Lake blossoms stole 64
Checkerboard tote bag 68
Japanese flower cushion 76
Cubist stool cover 82
Gipsy shawl 88
Big tea cozy 92
Lattice chair back throw 96
Chrysanthemum panel 100
Tumbling blocks panel 104
Jazz apron 110

Patchwork basics 116
Templates 122
Fabrics 124
Suppliers 126
Acknowledgments 128

Inspiration and ideas

As everyone knows, I just love color. Designing my fabrics in the Kaffe Fassett Collection for Westminster Fibers is something of a passion, and I look forward to each season and the opportunity to design new fabrics in the range, and to see the ideas my fellow designers come up with, too. My quilt books allow me, and the designers in my team, the chance to showcase these fabrics on a major scale.

But I am also aware that my patchwork fabrics can be used in different ways, too. Not everyone has the time or dedication to piece a quilt, beautiful and beguiling though it may be, and many people just love the fabrics but are not quite sure what they might do with them.

This book is simply a collection of ideas for smaller projects that nevertheless allow me to put colors and pattern contrasts together in ways that add a special spark to the design. Quite a few of the designs are very simply pieced together but others are a little more complex, but they are all, I hope, fun. What is more, they may inspire you to try out new ideas of your own with different fabrics, or with what is left in your stash.

You can use colorful small projects in your home in many different ways. You can, like me, pile color on color in a great adrenalin rush or you can use it sparingly to make a wonderfully rich accent in an otherwise tonal setting. But, to my way of thinking, color lifts the spirit and sets a different mood, and I will never get enough of it!

Kaffe Fassett

leafy apron

This eye-catching apron mixes flowers with stripes. A piece of wide ribbon is appliquéd to the apron just below the armholes. You cut out and join the strips for the binding (see page 119) before you start to make the apron.

MATERIALS
Apron fabric
Lotus Leaf   Antique   ⅞yd (80cm)

Ribbon
Roman Stripes   Pink & Blue   ¾yd (70cm)

Binding
Zig Zag   Cool   ¾yd (70cm)

Other materials
Pattern paper
Matching cotton thread

making the leafy apron

FINISHED APRON SIZE
Approx. 29 x 26in (73.5 x 66cm)

PREPARATION
Make a paper pattern following the diagram below. You can draw the curve freehand or use a rounded object, such as a plate, to draw around.
Note: pattern includes a double ⅝in (1.5cm) seam allowance.

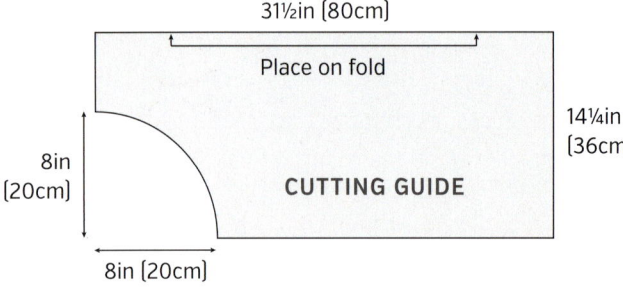

CUTTING OUT THE FABRIC
Fold the Lotus Leaf fabric in half on the grainline. Place the pattern with the straight side on the fold of the fabric. Pin and cut out.

To make bias binding strips (see page 119), fold the Zig Zag fabric on the bias and cut 2⅜in- (6cm-) wide strips until you have approx. 4yd (3.6m) of binding.

KAFFE FASSETT'S BRILLIANT LITTLE PATCHWORKS

SEWING THE APRON

Attaching the ribbon

1 Open out the Lotus Leaf fabric with RS facing. Pin the ribbon in place across the full width of the apron with the top edge of the ribbon ⅝in (1.5cm) down from the top of the sides. Match the side raw edges with the raw edge of the apron (A). Topstitch along the top and bottom edge of the ribbon to attach to the apron.

Hemming the sides and edge

2 Fold the bottom edge of the apron under by ⅝in (1.5cm) and then fold again by the same amount and press. Repeat for each straight side, folding the corners neatly and pinning in place (B). Machine sew in place.

A. Pinning the ribbon across the width of the apron top.

B. Folding and pinning the side and bottom edge double hem.

BINDING THE EDGES

Add the binding first to the apron top and then to the armhole edges to make the neck and waist ties.

Binding the top edge

3 Cut a 12½in (31.5cm) length of binding strip. With RS together, attach the binding to the top edge of the apron (see page 119), starting at one armhole edge, raw edges aligned (C). Trim the end level with the side of the apron.

4 Fold the binding over the raw edge. Pin and topstitch (see page 118) in place (D).

C. Attaching the binding strip to the top edge.

D. Topstitching the binding in place.

LEAFY APRON

Ties and armhole binding

5 Cut the remaining binding strip in half, fold in half again and mark the center with a pin. Match the pin with the bottom edge of the apron armhole. With RS facing and raw edges aligned, pin the binding in position, stretching it slightly so that it lies flat when stitched. Stitch in place along the fold (E).

6 Fold the binding to the wrong side of the armhole and pin through all layers from the front (F). Press the folded binding along the length of the ties. Fold in the ends of the ties by ¼in (6mm), then topstitch from the RS, along the waist tie, around the armhole, and continue to the end of the neck tie. Repeat on the other side.

E. Attaching the binding to the armhole.

F. Pinning before topstitching the length of the tie.

hexagon bolster

This little bolster is made up of small hexagons using five different fabrics, some in more than one colorway, but you could ring the color changes to suit your needs. I love the combination of the bright colors of the fussy cut flowers with the more sober geometric patterns. Making hexagon patchwork is a bit laborious as it requires careful cutting and stitching so that the hexagons fit together perfectly, but the result has great charm.

MATERIALS

Hexagon patchwork fabric

Guinea Flower	White	½yd (45cm)
Guinea Flower	Blue	¼yd (25cm)
Guinea Flower	Pink	¼yd (25cm)
Millefiore	Blue	¼yd (25cm)
Paperweight	Pastel	¼yd (25cm)
Spot	China Blue	¼yd (25cm)
Spot	Red	¼yd (25cm)
Aboriginal Dot	Lilac	¼yd (25cm)
Aboriginal Dot	Mint	¼yd (25cm)

Other materials

Template plastic
Freezer paper
2 x ¾in (2cm) self-cover buttons
Cotton sewing thread
Strong sewing thread
Short fine sewing needle
Bolster insert, 15 x 6in (38 x 15cm)
Long toy-making needle

KAFFE FASSETT'S BRILLIANT LITTLE PATCHWORKS

making the hexagon bolster

FINISHED BOLSTER SIZE
Approx. 14 x 6in (35 x 15cm)

PREPARATION
Copy the hexagon template A (see page 122) onto template plastic and use it to cut out 99 hexagons from freezer paper.

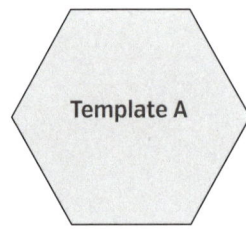

CUTTING OUT THE FABRIC
Cut out the fabric for the hexagons as follows to give a total of 99 hexagons.

Fussy cut (see page 116) 9: 2½in (6.5cm) squares from each of:
A Guinea Flower White
B Guinea Flower Blue
C Guinea Flower Pink
D Millefiore Blue
E Paperweight Pastel

Cut 18: 2½in (6.5cm) squares from:
F The background area of Guinea Flower White

Cut 9: 2½in (6.5cm) squares from each of:
G Spot China Blue
H Spot Red
I Aboriginal Dot Lilac
J Aboriginal Dot Mint

From the remaining Guinea Flower White, cut 2: 4 x 20½in (10 x 52cm) rectangles for the bolster ends. This includes a ⅝in (1.5cm) seam allowance.

SEWING THE HEXAGONS
1 Prepare the hexagons by placing each paper template centrally on the reverse side of each fabric square, and pin in the center. Paper-piece the fabric hexagons in place (see page 117). Each hexagon must be the same shape and size to fit together correctly (A).

A. Paper-piecing the hexagons.

2 When you have paper-pieced all 99 hexagons, lay out the hexagons in strips of 11, following the order shown in **Fig 1**. There will be nine strips.

3 Follow the instructions on page 117 to sew the paper-pieced hexagons together in strips, starting with the first two shapes, placing them with RS facing. Oversew the edges together with small even stitches (B).

B. Oversewing two paper-pieced hexagons.

16 KAFFE FASSETT'S BRILLIANT LITTLE PATCHWORKS

COMPLETING THE PATCHWORK PIECE

4 To sew the strips together, place the first pair of strips (1 and 2) together (C). Attach the thread on the WS of the work and oversew the first two edges together, RS facing, as in Step 2. Continue stitching corresponding edges together all along the strip. You will need to turn the strips and fold hexagons in half to allow the edges to meet.

5 Continue to add strips following the order and placement in Fig 1. Remove the basting and paper templates when all the pieces are sewn together.

C. Sewing strips together.

Fig 1. Order of piecing hexagons and strips.

HEXAGON BOLSTER

MAKING THE BOLSTER

6 To join the seam to create a cylinder, place the RS together and oversew the short edges together, folding the unstitched hexagons in half to allow the next part of the seam to be stitched. As shown, the hexagons fit together and the stripes join perfectly (E).

7 Fold each rectangle of fabric for the bolster ends so that the RS are facing and the raw edges of the short sides are aligned. Sew a ⅝in (1.5cm) seam to make a tube. Press the seam open.

8 With RS facing, line up the bolster seam with a seam between two hexagons on the edge of the tube, and insert one edge of the Guinea Flower White bolster end under the hexagons, so that 3⅜in (8.5cm) is showing at the widest point. Pin in place along the edge of the hexagons (F).

9 With a short, fine needle and matching thread, place the needle under the hexagon turning, bringing the needle out on the fold. Fasten on the thread with a couple of stitches and slip stitch or ladder stitch (see page 118) the two pieces together (G).

Repeat at the other end, remembering to align the seams on both bolster ends.

E. Joining the short edges to make a cylinder.

F. Pinning the bolster end in place.

G. Stitching the bolster ends.

KAFFE FASSETT'S BRILLIANT LITTLE PATCHWORKS

FINISHING THE BOLSTER ENDS

10 Insert the bolster pad. Turn under the bolster end fabric by enough so that the fabric reaches halfway across the diameter of the pad. Press the fold. Using a strong thread and a large knot, sew a row of gathering stitches along the edge (H). Draw up the gathering thread and secure in place.

H. Sewing gathering stitches along the bolster hem.

11 Repeat Step 10 at the other end. Cover the self-cover buttons with fabric (see page 120). Using a long doubled length of strong thread, and a toy-making needle, attach one button to the center of one bolster end (I).

I. Attaching a button to the bolster end.

12 Pass the thread through the length of the bolster. Rethread onto a sewing needle, pull to draw the ends of the bolster inward and make a small stitch to secure. Sew the second button in place. Fasten the thread securely.

HEXAGON BOLSTER 19

stripes cushions

These cushions make great use of my striped fabrics, playing with the geometry in the cutting out of the blocks, and playing with scale, too, mixing up bigger and smaller blocks. I created two colorways using the same piecing system for each, which starts with the big central block, made up of four large triangles, edged on two sides only with smaller blocks made from four smaller triangles.

How you place the triangle templates on the stripes determines the effect you get, so you can play with this idea to create your own versions.

I just love the way these blocks jump out at you and the fact that the cushions are not completely symmetrical.

MATERIALS

ARIZONA CUSHION
Patchwork fabric

Roman Stripe	Arizona	½yd (45cm)
Broad Stripe	Bliss	¼yd (25cm)

Cushion back fabric

Caterpillar Stripe	Sunshine	½yd (45cm)

BLOOD ORANGE CUSHION
Patchwork fabric

Roman Stripe	Blood Orange	½yd (45cm)
Broad Stripe	Watermelon	¼yd (25cm)

Cushion back fabric

Narrow Stripe	Red	½yd (45cm)

Other materials
Template plastic
Matching sewing thread
3 x ¾in (2cm) self-cover buttons, for each cushion

STRIPES CUSHIONS 21

making the stripes cushions

FINISHED CUSHION SIZE
Approx. 16 x 16in (40 x 40cm)

PREPARATION
You will need two sizes of template for the cushion. Copy Templates B and C on page 122 onto template plastic and cut out.

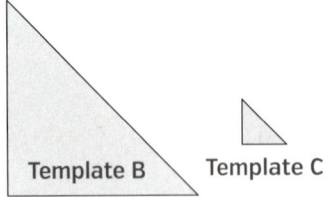

CUTTING OUT THE FABRIC
All measurements include a ¼in (6mm) seam allowance.

For the front
From Roman Stripe using Template B, cut 4 large triangles with the long side on the same color stripe.
From Broad Stripe using Template C, cut 7 sets of 4 small triangles (28 in total). Cut 4 triangles from each stripe so that each small block will be completely different.
Using Template C: cut 2 sets of 4 small triangles (8 in total), from a combination of both Roman Stripe and Broad Stripe. For each block use 2 triangles from each fabric.

For the back
From Caterpillar Stripe, cut 2: 16½ x 18½in (41.5 x 46.5cm) rectangles on the grainline.

22 KAFFE FASSETT'S BRILLIANT LITTLE PATCHWORKS

SEWING THE BLOCKS

The large and small blocks on the front of the cushion are made in the same way, combining 4 triangles to make a square block. Use a ¼in (6mm) seam allowance throughout, unless otherwise stated.

Front panel

1 For the large square, take two large triangles and place RS facing and pin the seam allowance along one short side, carefully matching the stripes across the seam (A). Sew the seam. Repeat with the remaining two large triangles. Press open the seams.

2 Open out the two pieces. Place the two halves of the block with RS facing, match and pin the center seam, matching the stripes (B), and sew the seam.

3 Press open the seams of the completed main block (C).

4 From the smaller triangles, make up 9 small squares following Steps 1–3, pressing the seams open.

A. Pinning triangles along the short diagonal seam.

B. Pinning the center seam along the two pieced halves.

C. Pressing the seams open on the completed block.

Pattern placement

Much of the charm of this design lies in the irregular placing of the fabrics for the small triangles, so don't worry too much about how you place the triangles on the striped fabric.

STRIPES CUSHIONS

ASSEMBLING THE BLOCKS

5 Arrange the completed smaller blocks as shown and join them together in one strip of 5 and one strip of 4 (D).

6 Place the strip of 4 blocks to the right side of the large panel, with RS facing. Stitch and press the seam open (E).

7 Place the strip of 5 blocks on the lower edge of the large panel, RS facing. Match the seam where the small square border joins the large panel. Stitch and press the seam open.

D. Laying out the blocks.

E. Attaching the strip of 4 to the main block.

MAKING THE CUSHION BACK

8 Follow the instructions on page 120 for making a buttoned cushion back, with 3 buttonholes. Use a ¼in (6mm) seam allowance when sewing around the edges of the cushion to keep the front squares correct.

9 Cover the self-cover buttons (see page 120) in Caterpillar Stripe fabric and mark the position of the buttons through the center of each buttonhole. Sew in place (F).

Alternatively, follow the instructions on page 120 for making a simple envelope back.

To make up the Blood Orange cushion variation, follow the instructions above, using the alternative colorway given in the materials list on page 21.

F. Attaching the buttons.

STRIPES CUSHIONS   25

summer flowers tablecloth

This wonderfully summery cloth is created from simple squares, cut from five different fabrics (some in more than one colorway), separated by sashing created from a little flowery print and edged with a double border of small and large print flowers.

MATERIALS
Patchwork panel

Millefiore	Lilac	¼yd (25cm)
Millefiore	Green	¼yd (25cm)
Lake Blossoms	Yellow	¼yd (25cm)
Lake Blossoms	Pink	¼yd (25cm)
Lake Blossoms	Green	¼yd (25cm)
Brassica	Yellow	¼yd (25cm)
Brassica	Pastel	¼yd (25cm)
Mad Plaid	Pastel	¼yd (25cm)
Mad Plaid	Mauve	¼yd (25cm)
Zig Zag	Pink	¼yd (25cm)

Sashing and borders

Guinea Flower	Mauve	2yd (1.8m)

Center border

Big Blooms	Duck Egg	1¾yd (1.6m)

Backing

Millefiore	Lilac	4yd (3.6m)

Other materials
Matching cotton thread

SUMMER FLOWERS TABLECLOTH

making the summer flowers tablecloth

FINISHED TABLECLOTH SIZE
Approx. 60 x 60in (153 x 153cm)

CUTTING OUT THE FABRIC

Patchwork squares
See diagram for cutting guide.

Border and sashing strips
When joining the border strips, keep the continuity of the design, for example by not cutting through flowers.

FROM GUINEA FLOWER MAUVE
Cut 22: 2½in (6.5cm) strips from the width of the fabric.

Outer border
Join four strips (taking care when joining the pattern). From the joined strip cut 2: 56½in (143.5cm) strips and 2: 60½in (154cm) strips.

Inner border
Join four more strips to make a single length. From the joined strip cut: 2: 46½in (118cm) strips and 2: 50½in (128.5cm) strips.

Sashing
From the remaining strips cut 5: 46½in (118cm) strips; cut 30: 6½in (16.5cm) strips from the remaining 2½in (6.5cm) strips, trimmed from the other strips, for the sashing rectangles.

FROM BIG BLOOMS DUCK EGG
Cut 8: 3½in (9cm) strips from the width of the fabric.

Center border
Join the strips in pairs (keeping the continuity of the flowers along the strip and centering the flowers on the width and length of the strip). From the joined strip cut 2: 50½in (128.5cm) strips and 2: 56½in (143.5cm) strips.

CUTTING GUIDE

KEY

Cut 36: 6½in (16.5cm) squares as follows:

A Millefiore Lilac x 3
B Millefiore Green x 3
C Lake Blossoms Yellow x 2
D Lake Blossoms Pink x 4
E Lake Blossoms Green x 2
F Brassica Yellow x 3
G Brassica Pastel x 5
H Mad Plaid Pastel x 2
I Mad Plaid Mauve x 3
J Zig Zag Pink x 4
K Big Blooms Duck Egg x 4

Borders

Guinea Flower Mauve
Big Blooms Duck Egg

SUMMER FLOWERS TABLECLOTH

SEWING THE PATCHWORK CENTRAL PANEL

Use a ¼in (6mm) seam allowance throughout, unless otherwise stated.

1 Following the diagram on page 28, lay out the squares in rows, as shown. Place a 6½in (16.5cm) sashing rectangle in between each of the 6 squares on every row.

2 Sew the squares and rectangles together to form each row (A). Complete the 6 rows of squares and rectangles.

3 Join the long sashing strips in between the 6 rows (B). Press the seams toward the sashing and trim the outer edges straight if necessary. You have now completed the central part of the tablecloth.

ATTACHING THE BORDERS

There are three borders: two narrower, same width inner and outer borders (Guinea Flower Lilac) and a wider central border (Big Blooms Duck Egg).

4 Following the instructions on page 118 for adding borders, method 2, add the inner border first (C). Trim any overhanging border ends so that the tablecloth is square.

5 Next, add the Big Blooms border using the same method as Step 4, and finally add the Guinea Flower outer border.

A. Sewing a sashing rectangle to a square.

B. Joining the sashing strips between the rows.

C. Adding the inner border.

BACKING AND FINISHING THE TABLECLOTH

6 Press the tablecloth. Check the size of the tablecloth top, it should measure 60½in (153cm) square. From the backing fabric, cut a 60½in (153cm) length (or length to match the finished size), and cut the remaining fabric in half lengthwise.

7 Cut off both selvedges from the full width length and turn under seam allowances of ⅝in (1.5cm). Match the pattern by placing the turned under edge over one of the halved lengths. Move around until the pattern matches exactly (D). Baste in place, then machine the seam. Repeat with the other side. The two half width lengths should align, top and bottom, depending on the pattern placement. Press open the seams. Cut a 60½in (153cm) square, or square to match the finished size of the top.

8 Place the backing and tablecloth top RS together. Sew together around the edge, using a ¼in (6mm) seam allowance, leaving a 6in (15cm) opening for turning through (see page 118).

9 Finger press the seam open on all four sides and then turn through to the RS. Slip stitch (see page 118) the opening closed (E) and press the edges.

10 To quilt the tablecloth, baste near to the seam joining the two borders and around the outer edge of the sashing that borders the squares (F). Then stitch in the ditch (see page 118) along the seams.

D. Matching the pattern on the seams on the back panel.

E. Slip stitching the opening.

F. Basting the borders before quilting.

SUMMER FLOWERS TABLECLOTH 31

brassica table runner

A very simple design, the impact comes from the huge flowers of my Brassica fabric, set off with a border in contrasting Guinea Flower. As with all simple designs, neat and accurate cutting and stitching is a must for a professional finish. The fabric for the central panel has to be pieced to make the length, with the longest length in the center of the runner, and two identical shorter ends. You need to take care to treat the fabric pattern sympathetically when cutting out the shorter ends.

MATERIALS

Central panel
Brassica	Green	½yd (50cm)

Border
Guinea Flower	Green	⅜yd (35cm)

Backing
Spot	Green	¾yd (70cm)

Other materials
Matching cotton thread

making the brassica table runner

FINISHED TABLE RUNNER SIZE
Approx. 60 x 12in (153 x 30cm)

CUTTING AND MAKING THE CENTRAL PANEL
All measurements include a ¼in (6mm) seam allowance.

1 From Brassica Green, cut 2: 8½in (21.5cm) strips across the width.

2 Fold one strip in half widthwise, cut along the fold, and position at either end of the second, whole strip (see Fig 1), placing the fabric to take the pattern into account–position the motifs so they remain whole or join two so that the design flows. Sew the three sections together and trim the seams to ⅝in (1.5cm). Press the seams open.

3 Fold the panel in half, so that the seams are lying on top of each other, and measure off 28¼in (72cm) from the fold. Cut off the excess fabric at each end.

CUTTING AND MAKING THE BORDERS
4 From Guinea Flower Green, cut 4: 2½in (6.5cm) strips across the width of the fabric. Join the strips into two pairs.

From each pair of strips, cut 1: 60½in (154.5cm) strip and 1: 8½in (21.5cm) strip.

Fig 1.

KAFFE FASSETT'S BRILLIANT LITTLE PATCHWORKS

MAKING THE TABLE RUNNER

Use a ¼in (6mm) seam allowance throughout, unless otherwise stated.

5 Follow the instructions on page 118 to add the borders using method 2. Add the Guinea Flower short border to each short end of the central panel (A). Press the seams toward the border.

6 Add the long side borders, pressing the seams toward the border.

BACKING AND FINISHING THE TABLE RUNNER

7 From Spot Green, cut 2: 12½in (31.5cm) strips across the width. Cut 1 strip in half lengthwise and, making sure that the seams will match the top of the table runner, join to either end of the center section. Press the table runner then place the backing on top so that RS are together.

8 Machine sew together, leaving a 6in (15cm) opening (see page 118). Trim off the excess fabric at the corners close to the stitching (B).

9 Finger press the seam open on all four sides and then turn through to the RS (C). Slip stitch the opening closed and press the edges.

10 To quilt the two layers together, use a matching thread to stitch in the ditch (see page 118) around the border.

A. Pinning the short border to the end of the central panel.

B. Trimming the corners.

C. Finger pressing the seam.

BRASSICA TABLE RUNNER

flower power kimono

For this kimono I have gone for a fabric design that packs a real punch for the main part of the garment, bordering it at the front with a contrasting flower fabric, and edging the sleeves with spotted fabric in two colors, and a contrasting ribbon. The result is a real statement piece. The collar of this kimono is lined with the same dark spot fabric that edges the sleeves. You can turn over the wide border and collar to create a shawl-style collar, revealing the contrast lining if you wish.

MATERIALS

Main fabric
Japanese Chrysanthemum Red   1¾yd (1.6m)

Collar band
Lake Blossoms   Black   ½yd (45cm)

Collar lining and Sleeve border
Spot   Black   ⅝yd (60cm)
Spot   Royal   ¼yd (25cm)

Lightweight woven interfacing
½yd (45cm)

Ribbon
Beach Ball   Black   1½yd (1.3m)

Other materials
Pattern paper
Matching cotton thread
1 x ¾in (2cm) self-cover button

36   KAFFE FASSETT'S BRILLIANT LITTLE PATCHWORKS

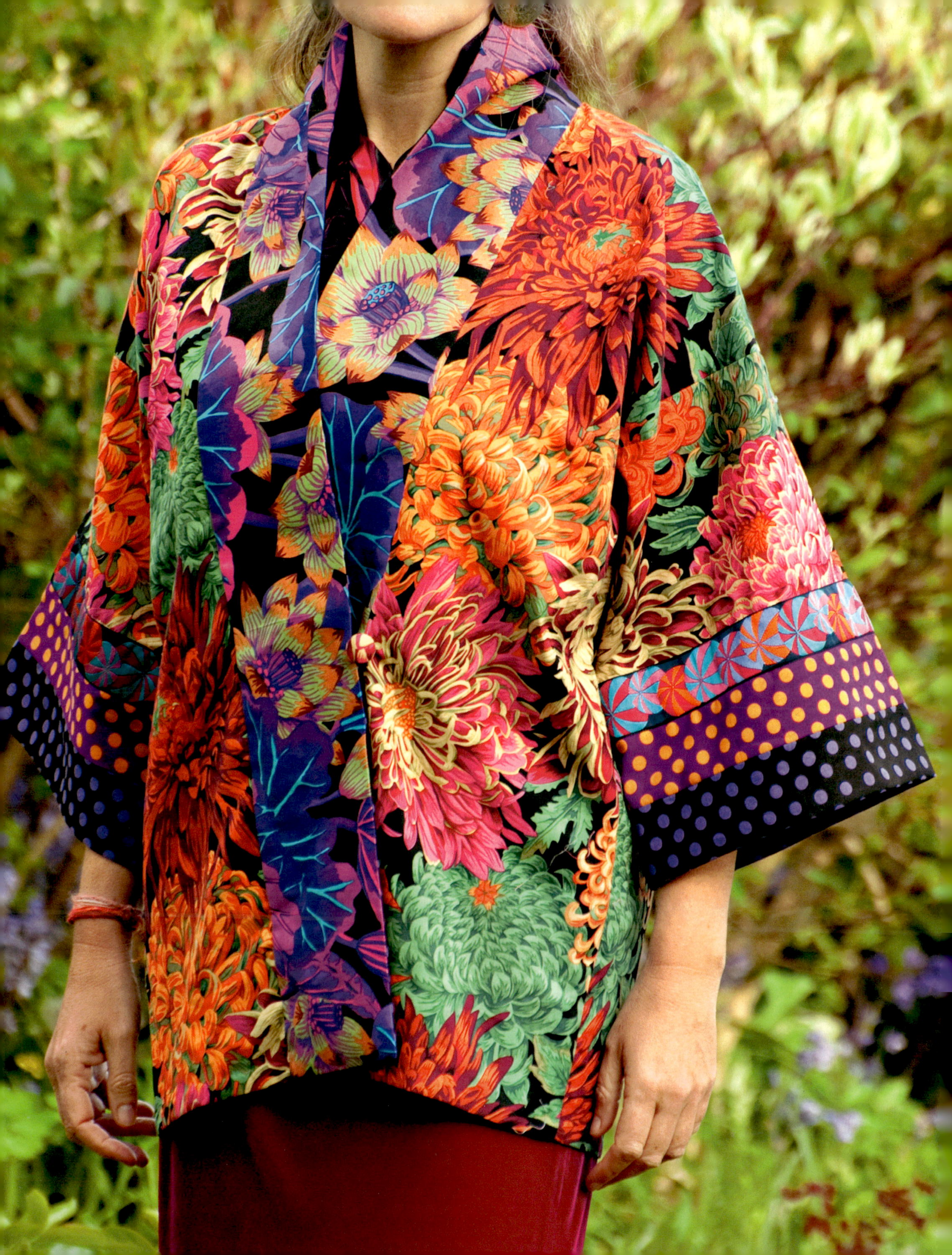

making the flower power kimono

FINISHED KIMONO SIZE
Length: approx. 28in (71.5cm)
Width across back: approx. 24in (61cm)

PREPARATION
Copy and cut out the pattern pieces following the diagrams right. To shape the back neck line, measure ⅝in (1.5cm) down from the top on the folded edge and mark. Draw a line from this mark and parallel to the top of the fabric measuring 3in (7.5cm) in from the fold. Measure 3in (7.5cm) in from the top right corner, and draw a line from this point down to the end of the first line, making a slim rectangle. To round off the corner, use a coin 1in (2.5cm) in diameter as a template to draw the curve. Transfer all marks to the pattern pieces.

CUTTING GUIDE

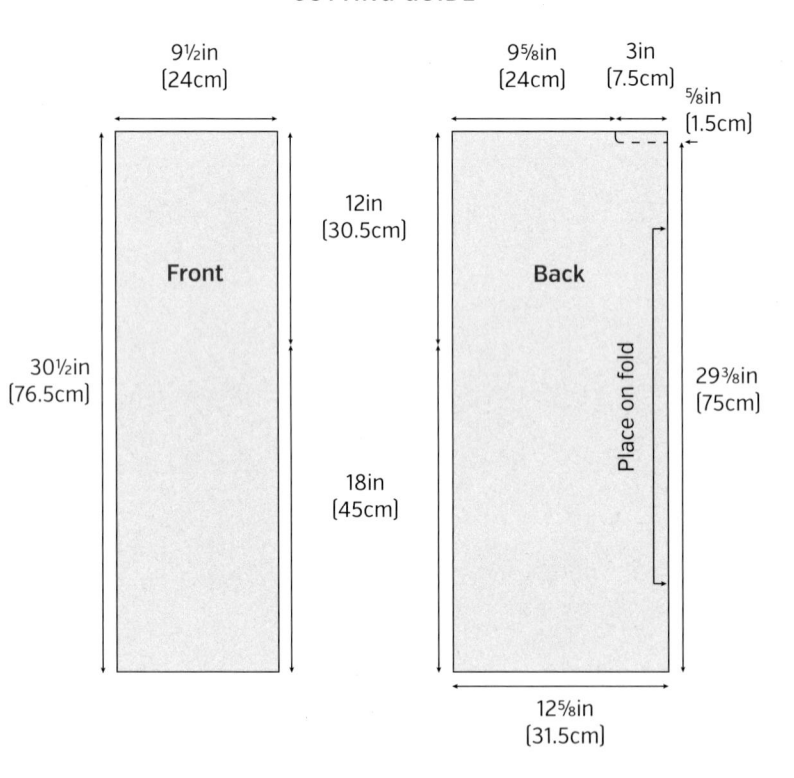

Front: 9½in (24cm) wide × 30½in (76.5cm) tall, with 12in (30.5cm) and 18in (45cm) sections.

Back: 9⅝in (24cm) + 3in (7.5cm) wide, ⅝in (1.5cm) from top, 29⅜in (75cm) tall, 12⅝in (31.5cm) at bottom, Place on fold.

CUTTING OUT THE FABRIC
All measurements include a ⅝in (1.5cm) seam allowance. Transfer all marks to the fabric pieces.

Japanese Chrysanthemum Red
Cut 1: back using the pattern piece, cut on the fold. At the neck edge make a small notch ¼in (6mm) into the seam allowance to match the collar seam.
Cut 2: fronts using the pattern piece.
Cut 2: 24 × 8¼in (61 × 21cm) rectangles, for sleeves. Mark the position of the shoulder seam at the center top edge of the sleeve.

Lake Blossoms Black
Cut 2: 33½ × 5¼in (85 × 13cm) rectangles, for collar band front.

Spot Black
Cut 2: 33½ × 5¼in (85 × 13cm) rectangles, for collar band lining.
Cut 2: 24 × 9in (61 × 23cm) rectangles, for sleeve borders.

Spot Royal
Cut 2: 24 × 3¼in (61 × 8.2cm) rectangles for sleeve borders.

Interfacing
Cut 2: 33½ × 5¼in (85 × 13cm) rectangles, for interfacing collar bands.

Beach Ball Black ribbon
Cut 2: 24in (61cm) lengths.

SEWING THE KIMONO

Back and front

1 With the RS facing, pin the shoulder seams together (from the sleeve edge to the neck) and stitch (A). Neaten the seams by turning under ¼in (6mm) and stitching.

Sleeves

2 With RS together, pin the Royal Spot border to the lower edge of the sleeve. Stitch in place, then sew the Black Spot border to the Royal Spot border. Press the seams open.

3 On the RS of the sleeve, place the ribbon just on the Japanese Chrysanthemum, slightly over the seam, pin, and topstitch in place (B). Repeat Steps 2 and 3 for the second sleeve.

4 At the top of the sleeve, fold the fabric to find the center and mark it. Line up the mark with the shoulder seam. Match the underarm marks to the marks on the side seam. Pin and stitch between the marks (C). Repeat with the second sleeve.

Side seam

5 Line up the side seams at the underarm, where the sleeve joins the front and back. Pin and stitch the side seams (D).

6 Then pin and stitch the sleeve seam. Neaten all seams by turning under ¼in (6mm) and edge stitching.

Sleeve hem

7 On the sleeve hem, turn the raw edge of the sleeve under by ⅝in (1.5cm) and then turn the border under to meet the seam line between the two spot fabrics. Slip stitch (see page 118) the hem in place on the WS of the seam allowance, between the top border and sleeve.

A. Pinning the shoulder seams.

B. Topstitching the ribbon.

C. Attaching the sleeve.

D. Stitching the side seams at the armhole.

FLOWER POWER KIMONO

Collar band

Join together the front collar fabric and the lining fabric before you attach these to the main fabric of the kimono, sandwiching the interfacing between the layers.

8 First, fuse the interfacing to the WS of the two Lake Blossoms collar band pieces, then join the two pieces with RS facing along the short seam. Join the two Spot collar band lining pieces in the same way and press seams open.

9 Place the Lake Blossoms front collar band RS facing up, with the flower design the correct way up. Position the Spot collar lining piece on top, RS together. Match the crossed seam at the center back (see page 117), pin all along the top of the collar and both short edges (**E**).

10 Begin stitching ⅝in (1.5cm) from the raw edge of one short side, along the top long edge, and finish ⅝in (1.5cm) from the raw edge on the opposite short side. Follow the instructions on page 118 for turning corners. Press the seam open.

11 Trim both the corners and trim the interfaced seam allowance by half. Finger press the seams open and trim the seam allowance to ¼in (6mm), all the way round the collar (**F**), including the extra fabric at the hem edge. Remove the corners.

Attaching the collar

12 Place the center back seam of the Lake Blossoms section RS together with the center back notch on the neck edge. Pin from the center back, along the back neck and front edges. The collar should be 1¼in (3cm) short of the front edge of the kimono. (This extra length allows for a ⅝in/1.5cm double hem.) Stitch in place. Clip the seam allowances around the neck. Press the seam allowance toward the collar. Fold the raw edge of the Spot lining under by ⅝in (1.5cm) and press (**G**).

E. Sewing the collar front and facing pieces RS together.

F. Trimming the seam allowance.

G. Attaching the collar.

Finishing the hem

13 Working from the WS, turn up the kimono hem level with the lower edge of the Lake Blossom collar border; this should be 1¼in (3cm), then fold the raw edge under to the crease. Press and slip stitch in place (H).

Collar band

14 Turn the collar through to the RS. Ensure that the corners are turned through correctly and press. Pin the collar facing in place and slip stitch to the collar seam.

Adding the button

15 Following the instructions on page 120, cover the self-cover button with Japanese Chrysanthemum Red. Sew the button in place on the collar seam between the waist and hip.

Making the buttonhole loop

16 Make a buttonhole loop on the back of the collar band in line with the button (I). Secure a double thread to the back of the edge where the button loop is required. Once the thread is secure make your loop by creating five to six long stitches in the same place–the stitch length needs to be the same as the button diameter. Lay the thread to the left of the stitches. Pass the blunt end of the needle under the stitches and over the thread, pull the thread toward the end of the stitches (J). A knot will form at the end. Continue until the length of the loop stitches are covered with knots. Fasten off the thread.

H. Slip stitching the hem.

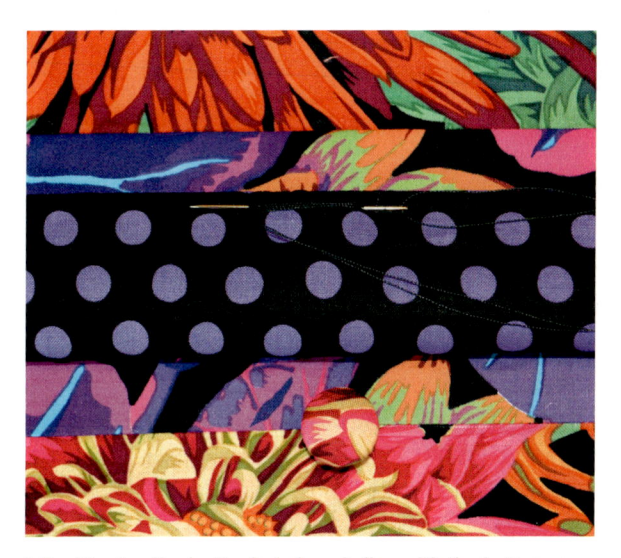

I. Positioning the buttonhole loop in line with the button.

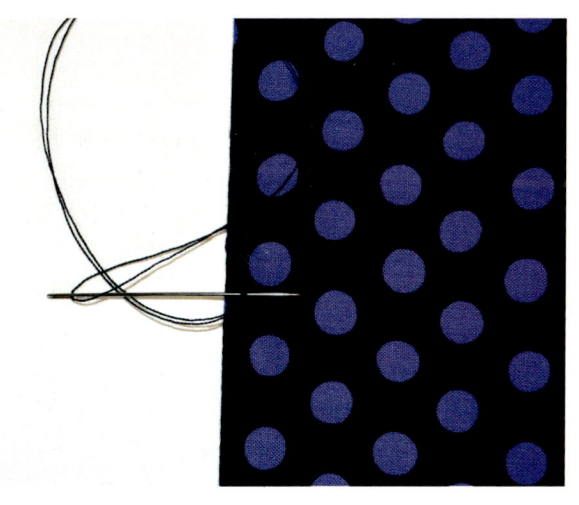

J. Sewing a buttonhole loop.

FLOWER POWER KIMONO

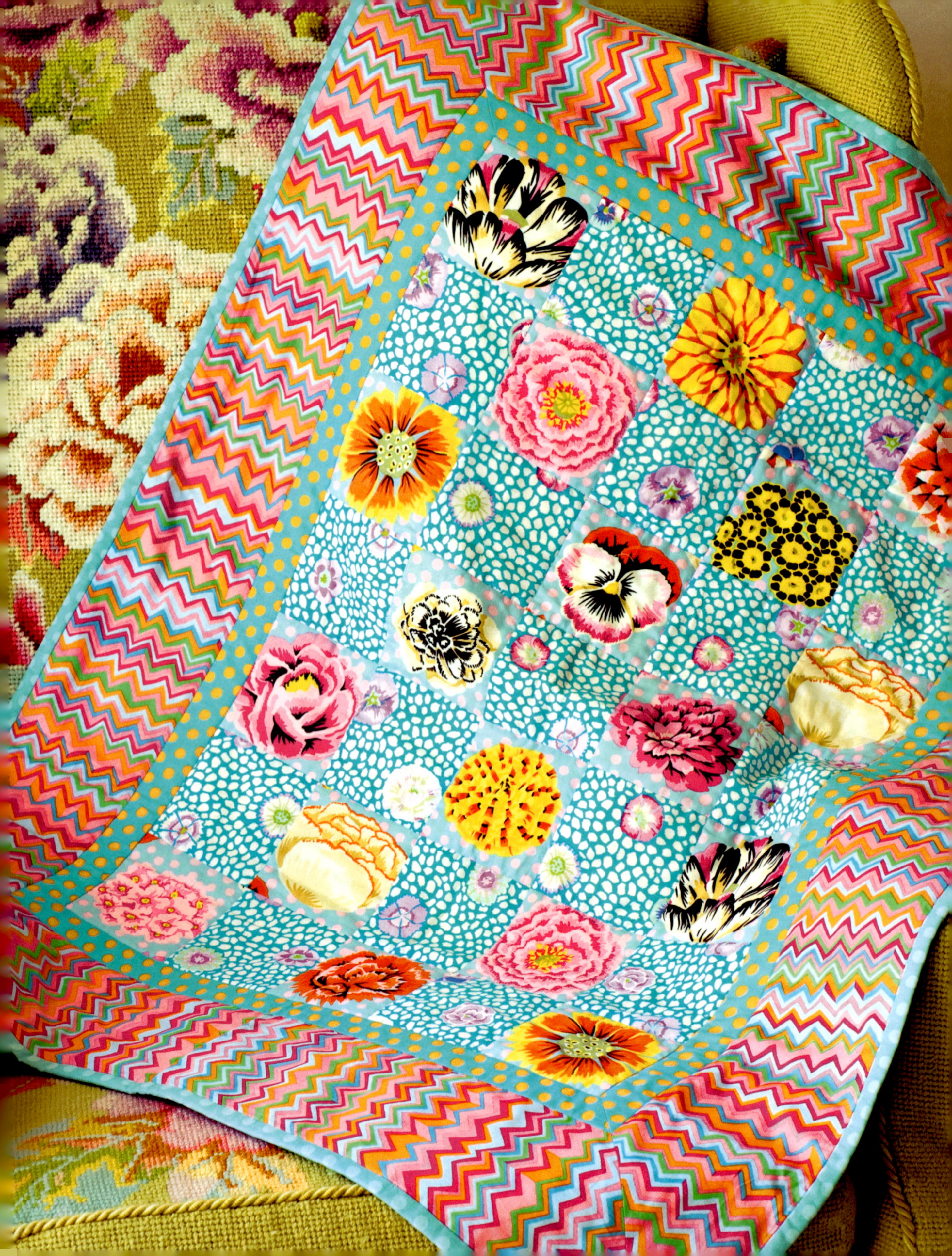

big blooms miniquilt

This very pretty little quilt doubles up: it would look delightful in a small girl's room but it would make a lovely knee rug, too, for a sun room perhaps. The design is simple—a central panel made up of large fussy cut flower squares alternating with a small flower print. This is edged with a narrow spot border surrounded by wider Zig Zag stripe, and bound with spot fabric.

MATERIALS
Central panel
Guinea Flower	Turquoise	⅜yd (35cm)
Big Blooms	Duck Egg	¾yd (70cm)

Border
Spot	Turquoise	¼yd (25cm)
Zig Zag	Pink	1¼yd (115cm)

Backing fabric
Millefiore	Lilac	1¼yd (115cm)

Binding
Spot	China Blue	¼yd (25cm)

Batting
46 x 38in (117 x 96.5cm)

Other materials
Quilter's rule and tailor's chalk or a fading marker
Matching cotton thread

BIG BLOOMS MINIQUILT 43

making the big blooms miniquilt

FINISHED QUILT SIZE
Approx. 41 x 33in (104 x 84cm)

CUTTING OUT THE FABRIC
All measurements include a ¼in (6mm) seam allowance.

Central panel
From Guinea Flower Turquoise, cut 17: 4½in (11.2cm) squares.
From Big Blooms Duck Egg, fussy cut (see page 116) 18: 4½in (11.2cm) squares.

Borders
From Spot Turquoise, cut 4: 2in (5cm) wide strips across the width of the fabric.
From Zig Zag Pink, cut 4: 5½in (14cm) wide strips from the length of the fabric (45in/115cm).

Backing
From Millefiore Lilac, cut 1: 45 x 37in (116 x 95cm) rectangle.

Binding
From Spot Duck Egg, cut 4: 2in (5cm) strips across the width of the fabric. Follow the instructions on page 119 to make a length of binding 4½yd (4.1m) long.

CUTTING GUIDE

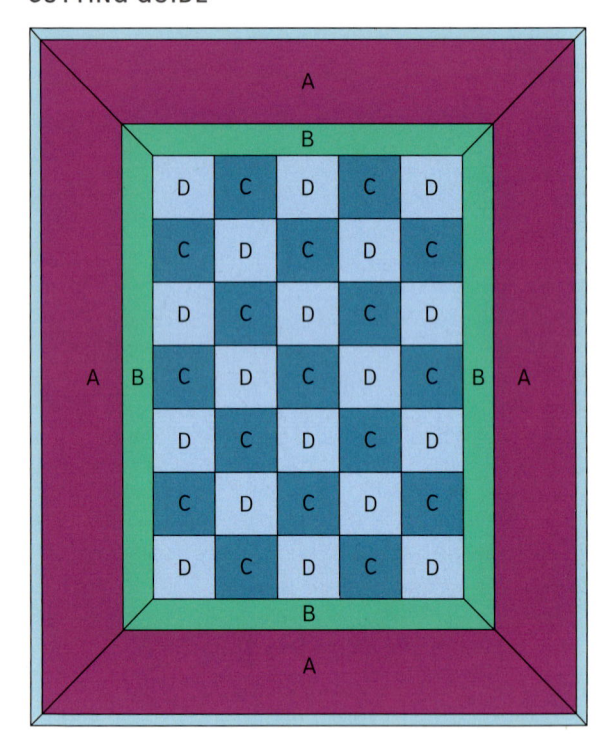

KEY

- Spot Duck Egg
- A Zig Zag Pink
- B Spot Turquoise
- C Guinea Flower Turquoise
- D Big Blooms Duck Egg

BIG BLOOMS MINIQUILT 45

MAKING THE QUILT

Use a ¼in (6mm) seam allowance throughout, unless otherwise stated.

ASSEMBLING THE CENTRAL PANEL

1 Lay out the squares in rows of 5 (A), alternating the placement of the Big Blooms squares as shown in the diagram on page 44. Join the squares together (see page 117) so that you have 7 strips.

2 Join the strips together, placing the first two strips RS together and matching the seams. Join each strip in order (B). Press the seams open. Press the patchwork panel.

A. Joining squares together to make strips.

B. Sewing strips right sides together to make the central panel.

ATTACHING THE MITERED BORDERS

3 Starting with the Spot side borders, begin pinning a strip to the edge, following the instructions for adding mitered borders on page 119. Fold the panel diagonally across the center. Using a ruler, extend the 45-degree line from the fold across the border and mark with tailor's chalk or a fading marker. Pin and stitch the seam, then trim away the excess fabric. Repeat for the remaining three corners.

4 Following the method in Step 3, attach the Zig Zag borders, again begin from the center of each strip and work toward the corners (C) and (D).

C. Attaching the Zig Zag borders.

D. The two borders in position.

BACKING AND FINISHING THE QUILT

5 Press the quilt top. Place RS down and layer the quilt with the batting and the backing fabric, RS facing up. Baste the layers together (see page 120).

6 To quilt the top, stitch in the ditch (see page 118) with matching thread on all seams (E).

7 Trim the batting and the backing fabric. Following the instructions on page 119 for mitered binding, attach the binding to the edge of the quilt. Turn the folded edge of the binding to the back of the quilt and slip stitch in place (see page 118).

E. Quilting with "stitch in the ditch" on all seams.

BIG BLOOMS MINIQUILT

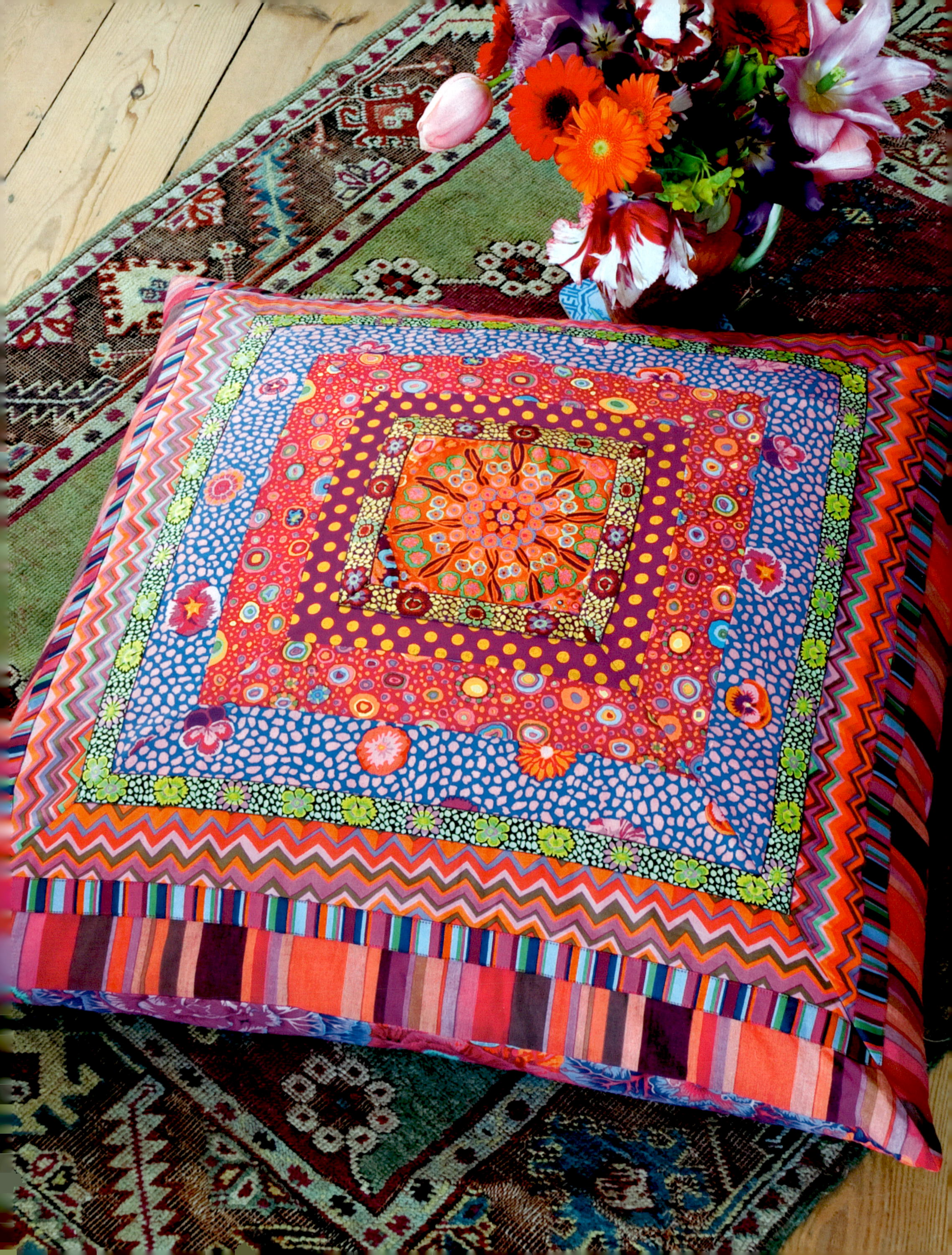

fiesta floor cushion

I love the contrast of bright, hot colors in this generously sized cushion. I used both geometric and floral fabrics and added some of my ribbons for good measure. The design is based on a brightly colored central square, edged with borders of varying widths, in a range of vibrant contrasting colors.

MATERIALS

Borders

Spot	Magenta	¼yd (25cm)
Roman Glass	Red	¼yd (25cm)
Guinea Flower	Pink	¼yd (25cm)
Zig Zag	Warm	½yd (45cm)
Roman Stripe	Blood Orange	½yd (45cm)

Central square

Millefiore	Tomato	¼yd (25cm)

Ribbon

Guinea Flower	Plum	⅞yd (80cm)
Guinea Flower	Green	2½yd (2.3m)
Roman Stripes	Pink & Blue	3yd (2.75m)

Backing

Brassica	Red	1yd (90cm)

Other materials

Matching cotton thread
7 x ¾in (2cm) self-cover buttons
1 x 30in (76.5cm) square cushion form (pad)

making the fiesta floor cushion

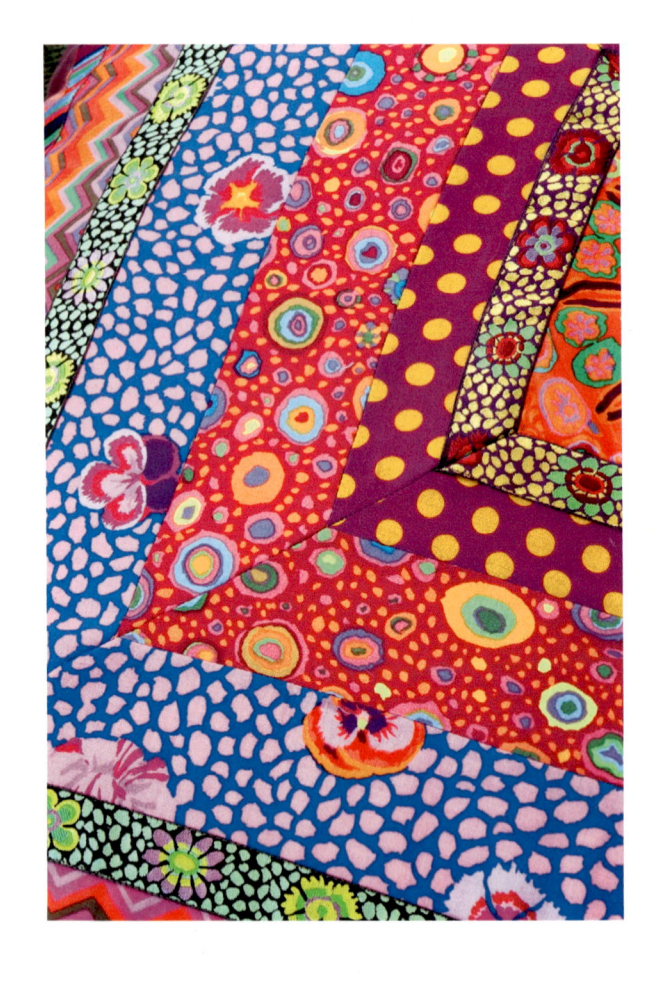

FINISHED FLOOR CUSHION SIZE
Approx. 30 x 30in (76.5 x 76.5cm) square

CUTTING OUT THE FABRIC
All measurements include a ¼in (6mm) seam allowance.

Borders
From Spot Magenta (A), cut 4: 2½ x 11¼in (6.5 x 28.6cm) strips.
From Roman Glass Red (B), cut 4: 2½ x 15¼in (6.5 x 38.8cm) strips.
From Guinea Flower Pink, (C) cut 4: 3 x 20¼in (7.5 x 51.5cm) strips.
From Zig Zag Warm (D) , cut 4: 3 x 25¼in (7.5 x 64.2cm) strips.
From Roman Stripe Blood Orange (E), cut 4: 3½ x 31¼in (9 x 79.4cm) strips.
To be able to join the patchwork sections with a diagonal seam, trim off the ends at a 45-degree angle. Be very accurate!

Central square
From Millefiore Tomato, fussy cut (see page 116) 1: 6½in (16.5cm) square.

Backing
From Brassica Red, cut 1: 32 x 30½in (81 x 77.5cm) rectangle; cut 1: 8 x 30½in (20 x 77.5cm) rectangle.

KEY
- A Spot Magenta
- B Roman Glass Red
- C Guinea Flower Pink
- D Zig Zag Warm
- E Roman Stripe Blood Orange

CUTTING GUIDE

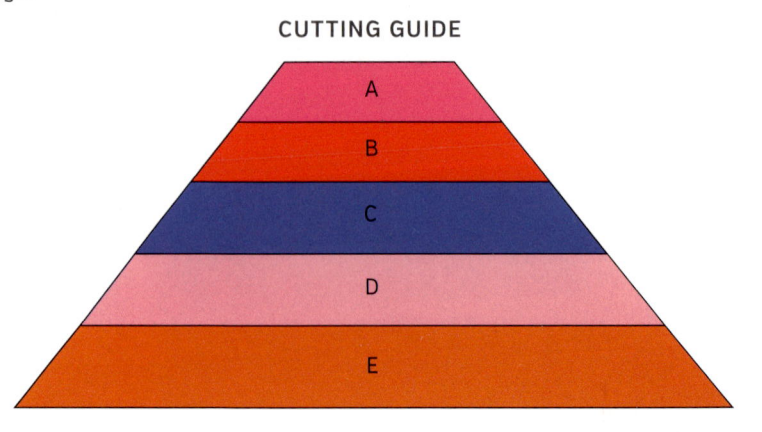

KAFFE FASSETT'S BRILLIANT LITTLE PATCHWORKS

FIESTA FLOOR CUSHION 51

SEWING THE TOP COVER

Use a ¼in (6mm) seam allowance throughout, unless otherwise stated.

First quarter section patchwork

Sew the top cover patchwork first, in four quarter sections, each identical.

1 Begin by joining the Fabric A strip to the Fabric B strip, following the instructions in the box below.

2 Continue to add strips, joining Fabric C to Fabric B, Fabric D to Fabric C, Fabric E to Fabric D (A).

3 Make up the other three quarter sections in the same way with the remaining strips of fabric. Press the seams open (B).

A. Joining strips.

B. Completed quarter pieced section.

Joining angled strips

Place the matching raw edges together with RS facing. At each end on the seam edge there will be an overlap with small triangles jutting out on each end from the shorter strip. Where the strips meet there is a "V." This is ¼in (6mm) from the edge and is your seam line. Sew the seam to join the two pieces. Add the next strip to the unstitched edge in the same way.

¼in (6mm) seam

52   KAFFE FASSETT'S BRILLIANT LITTLE PATCHWORKS

Attaching patchwork to central square

4 On the WS of the central square mark a small dot at each corner, ¼in (6mm) in from the edge.

5 Attach the short edge of each quarter section to each side of the central square, pinning each between the two dots on each side, leaving a ¼in (6mm) seam allowance at each end as you stitch (C).

C. Attaching a quarter section to the central square.

ADDING RIBBON APPLIQUÉ

6 Cut the Guinea Flower Plum ribbon into four pieces, each 8in (20cm) long. Place the ribbon over the Fabric A strip, so that it just covers the seam between the central square and Fabric A border (D).

7 Pin in place and topstitch both long sides of the ribbon. Trim the ribbon to match the edge of the fabric. Repeat to attach the remaining 3 pieces of ribbon.

8 Following Steps 6 and 7, apply the Guinea Flower Green ribbon to the Fabric C borders. Repeat with the Roman Stripes ribbon and place over the Fabric E border.

D. Attaching the ribbon trim.

FIESTA FLOOR CUSHION

FINISHING THE TOP COVER

9 To join the diagonal seams between the quarter sections, fold the panel diagonally across the central square. Pin each seam carefully, so that the border seams match (**E**).

10 Stitch the diagonal seams from the corner toward the central square. Your seam should finish at the point where the other two seams meet. Press seams open.

11 Repeat to join the remaining diagonal seams, folding the central panel in the opposite direction (**F**).

12 If the ends of the ribbon do not want to lie flat, put a couple of hand stitches in to hold them down.

MAKING THE CUSHION BACK

13 Place the WS of the large backing piece facing up, with the 30½in (78.8cm) edge horizontal. Fold up the lower edge by 4in (10cm) and crease the fold. Then fold under the raw edge to the crease. Pin and edge stitch the turning (**G**).

14 Repeat with the smaller section, folding the top edge down by 4in (10cm) and again fold under and edge stitch the turning.

15 Mark the positions of the seven buttonholes on the large section (parallel to the edge, within the turning) and machine stitch. Cut them open carefully.

E. Pinning the diagonal seam.

F. Joining the remaining seams.

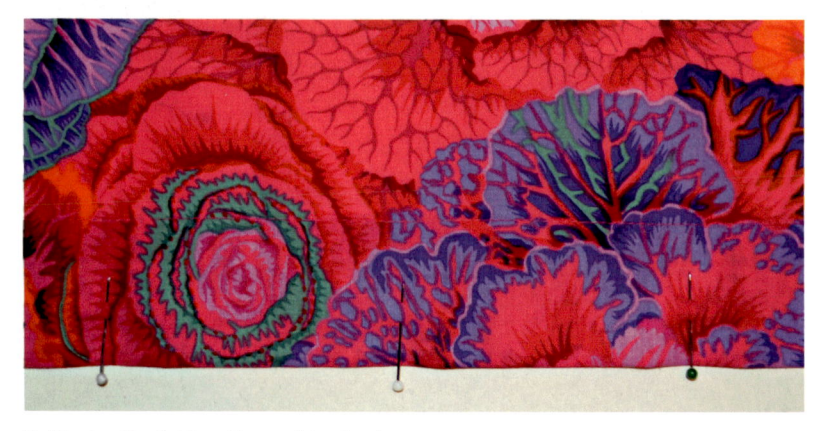

G. Pinning the fold on the cushion back.

SEWING THE FRONT AND BACKS TOGETHER

16 Lay the cushion front with RS facing up and place the larger back panel on top with RS together. The buttonholes will be toward the lower edge. Line up the three raw edges (H).

17 Put the smaller back section at the bottom, WS facing up, so that the turnings lie on top of each other and the raw edges are aligned. Pin and stitch around the cushion cover. Trim the seam allowance and clip the corners. Turn through and press.

H. Sewing the cushion back in place.

BUTTONS

18 Cover seven self-cover buttons (see page 120), each with different fabrics. Mark the position of the buttons through the center of each buttonhole (I) and sew in place (J). Insert the cushion form.

Alternatively, follow the instructions on page 120 for making a simple envelope back.

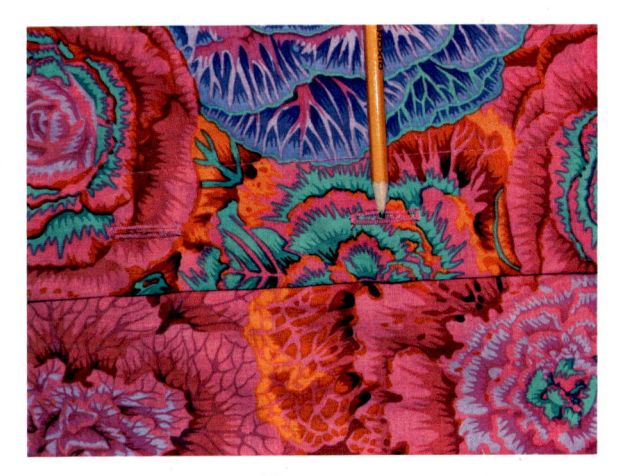

I. Marking the button positions.

Alternative fastenings

If you don't fancy covering buttons, then use up your stash of buttons, picking similar-sized buttons in bright colors that contrast with the backing fabric. And, if you don't want to make buttonholes, you could make button loops instead (like the one on the Kimono on page 41), remembering to make sure the loop is long enough to fit the diameter of the buttons and using a double thread (or strong button thread).

J. Sewing the buttons in place.

FIESTA FLOOR CUSHION 55

56

blues table runner and mats

For this set of a runner and mats, I chose different geometric prints in a range of blues. Both the runner and the mats are interlined and quilted; the runner quilted "in the ditch," and the mats in a trellis pattern across the central fabric.

MATERIALS FOR THE RUNNER

Borders
Aboriginal Dot	Iris	¼yd (25cm)
Spot	China Blue	¼yd (25cm)

Central panel
Roman Glass	Blue	¼yd (25cm)
Spot	Sky	¼yd (25cm)

Backing
Guinea Flower	Blue	⅜yd (35cm)

Heat resistant interlining
½yd (45cm)

Other materials
Matching cotton thread

MATERIALS TO MAKE FOUR MATS

Central panel
Roman Glass	Blue	¼yd (25cm)

Border
Aboriginal Dot	Iris	⅜yd (35cm)

Backing
Guinea Flower	Blue	⅜yd (35cm)

Heat resistant interlining
½yd (45cm)

Binding
Spot	China Blue	¼yd (25cm)

Other materials
Matching cotton thread

BLUES TABLE RUNNER AND MATS

making the blues table runner

FINISHED TABLE RUNNER SIZE
Approx. 32 x 12in (81.6 x 30.4cm)

CUTTING OUT THE FABRIC
All measurements include a ¼in (6mm) seam allowance.

Central panel
From Roman Glass Blue, cut 10: 3in (7.6cm) squares.
From Spot Sky, cut 10: 3in (7.6cm) squares.

Borders
From Aboriginal Dot Iris, cut 2: 2¼in (5.6cm) strips from the width of the fabric.
From each strip, cut 2: 25½in (65.2cm) strips and cut 2: 9in (22.8cm) strips.

From Spot China Blue, cut 2: 2¼in (5.6cm) strips from the width of the fabric.
From each strip, cut 2: 29in (74cm) strips and cut 2: 12½in (31.6cm) strips.

CUTTING GUIDE

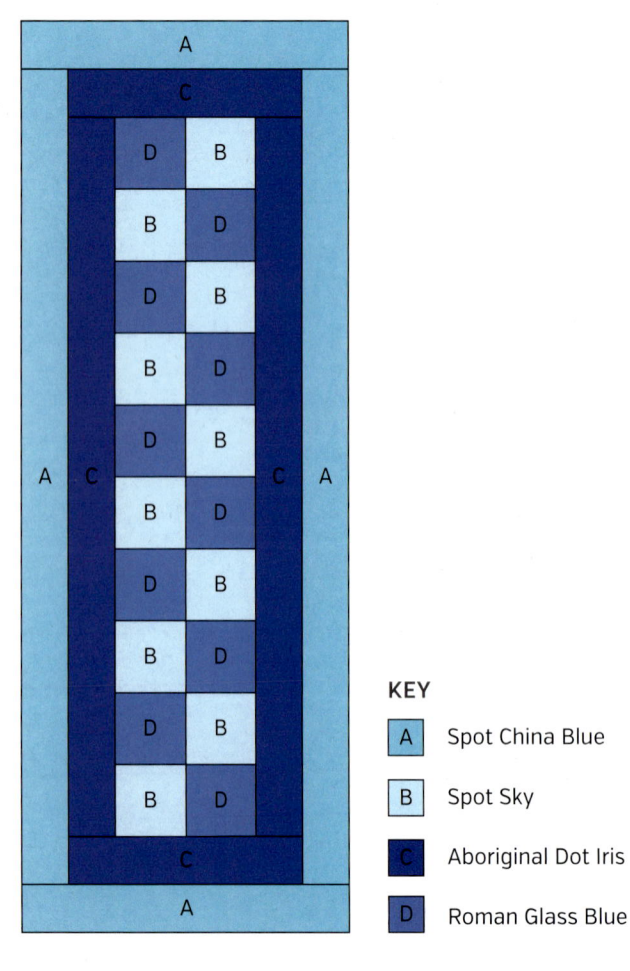

KEY
- A Spot China Blue
- B Spot Sky
- C Aboriginal Dot Iris
- D Roman Glass Blue

KAFFE FASSETT'S BRILLIANT LITTLE PATCHWORKS

MAKING THE CENTRAL PANEL

Use a ¼in (6mm) seam allowance throughout, unless otherwise stated.

1 Stitch alternating squares of each fabric RS together to create a row of 10 squares (**A**). Repeat with a second row. Press seams open.

2 Position the two strips next to each other so that the squares also alternate between the rows. Pin the two strips, RS together, taking care to match the seams (see page 117), and sew the seam (**B**). Press the seams open.

A. Stitching squares together to make a row.

B. Stitching the strips together.

ATTACHING THE BORDERS
Inner borders

3 Attach the Aboriginal Dot Iris borders, following the instructions on page 118 method 2, but sewing the long sides first (**C**). Press the seams toward the border.

4 Add the two short borders to the short ends and press the seams toward the border.

C. Attaching the long side borders.

BLUES TABLE RUNNER AND MATS

Outer borders

5   Repeat Steps 3 and 4 to add the Spot China Blue outer borders, adding the long side borders first, then the short ends (D). Press the seams toward the border and then press the finished table runner top on the RS.

D. Adding the short borders.

BACKING AND FINISHING THE TABLE RUNNER

6   Check the size of the top, it should measure 32½ x 12½in (82.8 x 31.6cm). From the backing fabric, cut a 32½ x 12½in (82.8 x 31.6cm) rectangle (or piece to match the finished size).

7   Place the backing and top with RS together and raw edges aligned. Sew a ¼in (6mm) seam around the edge, leaving a 6in (15cm) opening (see page 118), so that the runner can be turned through. Trim off the excess fabric at the corners close to the stitching (E).

E. Backing sewn in place and corners trimmed.

8   Finger press the seams open, turn the table runner to the right side, and press. Cut the heat resistant interlining to fit inside the table runner: 32 x 12in (81.6 x 30.4cm) or the final dimensions of your runner. Insert the interlining through the opening (F). Arrange the seam allowance so that it lies under the interlining.

9   Slip stitch the opening closed (see page 118) and press. To quilt the top, using a matching thread, stitch in the ditch (see page 118) on the seams between the borders.

F. Inserting the interlining.

61

making the blues table mats

FINISHED TABLE MAT SIZE
Approx. 12 x 9in (30.4 x 22.8cm)

CUTTING OUT THE FABRIC
All measurements include a ¼in (6mm) seam allowance.

Central panels
From Roman Glass Blue, cut 4: 8½ x 5½in (21.6 x 14cm) rectangles.

Borders
From Aboriginal Dot Iris, cut 4: 2¼in (5.6cm) strips from the width.
From each strip, cut 2: 8½in (21.6cm) strips and cut 2: 9½in (24cm) strips.

Backing
From Guinea Flower Blue, cut 4: 12 x 9in (30.4 x 22.8cm) rectangles.
Fom heat resistant interlining, cut 4: 12 x 9in (30.4 x 22.8cm) rectangles.

Binding
From Spot China Blue, cut 4: 2in (5cm) strips from the width. Join the strips (see page 119); the binding strip will be long enough to edge 4 table mats.

ATTACHING THE BORDERS
Use a ¼in (6mm) seam allowance throughout, unless otherwise stated.

1 Follow the instructions on page 118 method 2, but add the Aboriginal Dot border to each long side of the central panel rectangle first (A). Press seams toward the border.

2 Add the short borders to each short side (B). Press seams toward the border. Press the table mat top.

A. Adding the long side borders.

B. Adding the short borders.

KAFFE FASSETT'S BRILLIANT LITTLE PATCHWORKS

BACKING AND BINDING THE TABLE MAT

3 Press the table mat top and place RS down and layer the quilt with the batting and the backing fabric, RS facing up. Baste the quilt layers together, following the instructions on page 120. Trim the edges from the interlining and backing fabric.

4 With RS facing, attach the length of binding around the table mat (C), following the instructions on page 119 for binding with mitered corners.

5 Turn the folded edged of the binding to the back of the table mat and slip stitch (see page 118) in place (D), mitering the corners.

C. Attaching the binding.

D. Slip stitching the binding to the back.

FINISHING THE TABLE MAT

6 Using matching thread, stitch in the ditch (see page 118) around the border and quilt diagonally on the center panel, following the quilting diagram (see Fig 1).

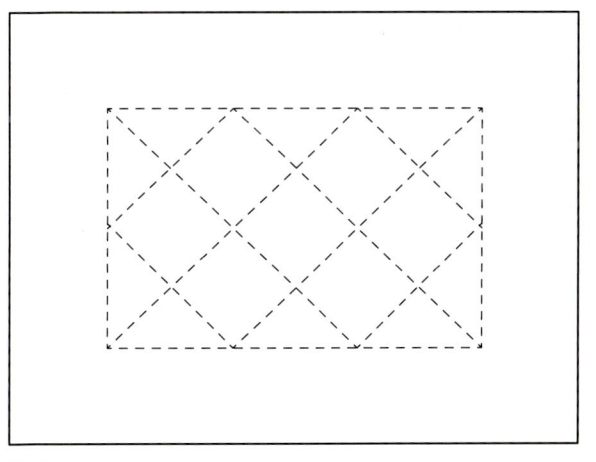

Fig 1.

BLUES TABLE RUNNER AND MATS

64

lake blossoms stole

I love the way the brilliant blues and pinks simply dance across this stole. The central panel is created from eye-catching blousy Lake Blossoms flowers, bordered with a narrow spot border and a wider one from Ombre, in which the colors change within the fabric itself. As a finishing touch, I embroidered rows of long running stitches in a toning color.

MATERIALS

Lake Blossoms	Blue	1¾yd (1.6m) or ½yd (45cm)
Spot	Sapphire	1¾yd (1.6m) or ¼yd (25cm)
Ombre	Blue	¼yd (25cm)

Backing

Millefiore	Blue	1¾yd (1.6m) or ¾yd (70cm)

See Cutting Guide for alternative piecing using less fabric.

Other materials

Matching cotton thread
Anchor stranded embroidery silk in matching shade
Embroidery needle

LAKE BLOSSOMS STOLE

making the lake blossoms stole

FINISHED STOLE SIZE
Approx. 60 x 11in (1.53m x 28cm)

CUTTING OUT THE FABRIC
Front
From Lake Blossoms, cut 1: 61¼ x 7¼in (156 x 18cm) rectangle from the length; or cut 2 strips across the width and piece together, cutting to the required length.
From Spot, cut 1: 61¼ x 3¼in (156cm x 8cm) rectangle from the length; or cut 2 strips across the width and piece together, cutting to the required length.
From Ombre, cut 2: 4¼in (11cm) strips from across the width. Join the short ends of the Ombre strips together, matching the pattern if possible. Then cut to a length of 61¼in (156cm).

Backing
From Millefiore, cut 1: 61¼ x 12¼in (156 x 31cm) rectangle; or cut 2 strips across the width and piece together, cutting to the required length.

SEWING THE FRONT
Use a ⅝in (1.5cm) seam allowance throughout, unless otherwise stated.

1 With RS facing, place the Spot on the left-hand side of the Lake Blossoms rectangle, aligning the long edges. Pin and stitch.

2 Attach the Ombre rectangle on the right-hand side of the Lake Blossoms. Press both seams open (A).

JOINING THE FRONT AND BACK
3 Pin the front to the backing with RS together (B), leaving a 4in (10cm) opening to turn the scarf through.

A. Pressing seams open on both borders.

B. Pinning the backing in place, RS together.

KAFFE FASSETT'S BRILLIANT LITTLE PATCHWORKS

FINISHING THE BACKING

4 Following the instructions on page 118 for turning corners and sewing openings, sew the pieces together.

5 Trim away the corners to reduce the bulk (C) and finger press the seam open all the way round, including the opening.

C. Trimming the corners before turning through.

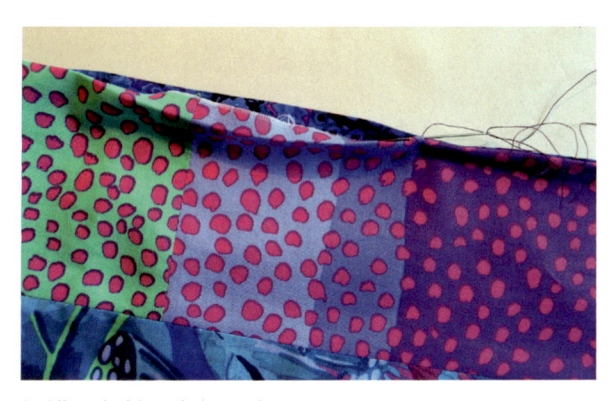

D. Slip stitching the opening.

6 Remove the large stitches across the opening and turn the scarf through, teasing out the corners. Slip stitch or ladder stitch (see page 118) the opening (D). Press.

ADDING EMBROIDERY

7 On the front of the scarf, add lines of running stitch (see box) in matching embroidery silk, starting ¼in (6mm) in from each edge and evenly spaced in between (E). You can either work the rows by eye, or mark out the lines first with a fading fabric marker, dividing the width into approximately 12 lines.

E. Adding rows of running stitch.

Running stitch

To work running stitch, working from right to left, secure the thread with a small stitch and bring the needle out on the stitch line, insert it a stitch length along and bring it out again a stitch length ahead. Continue to sew even-sized stitches at regular intervals along the stitch line.

LAKE BLOSSOMS STOLE

checkerboard tote bag

Four different colors of Spot fabric create the front and back checkerboard-style squares of this tote bag, while a mixture of Aboriginal Dot and Spot fabrics form the gussets and strap, which is appliquéd with toning Plink ribbon, adding to its strength and its impact.

MATERIALS

(A)	Spot	Magenta	¼yd (25cm)
(B)	Spot	Royal	¼yd (25cm)
(C)	Spot	Black	¼yd (25cm)
(D)	Spot	Green	⅜yd (35cm)
(E)	Aboriginal Dot	Purple	¼yd (25cm)

Lining
Paperweight   Purple   ⅝yd (60cm)

Ribbon (optional)
Plink   Black   2yd (1.8m)

Woven fusible interfacing
½yd (45cm)

Other materials
Matching cotton thread
Stiff card or cardboard (optional)

68   KAFFE FASSETT'S BRILLIANT LITTLE PATCHWORKS

69

making the checkerboard tote bag

FINISHED BAG SIZE
Approx. 14 x 14in (36.4 x 36.4cm), excluding handles

CUTTING OUT THE FABRIC
All measurements include a ¼in (6mm) seam allowance.

Patchwork squares
Cut strips of fabric across the width then cut the strips into the number of squares required (see diagram).
From fabric A, cut 1: 2½in (6.4cm) strip.
From fabric B, cut 3: 2½in (6.4cm) strips.
From fabric C, cut 2: 2½in (6.4cm) strips.
From fabric D, cut 3: 2½in (6.4cm) strips.
From fabric E, cut 2: 2½in (6.4cm) strips.

Lining
From Paperweight Purple, cut 1: 2½in (6.4cm) strip across the width, then cut 1: 34½in (89.6cm) length, for the strap.
Cut 2: 2½in (6.4cm) strips across the width, then cut 2: 21½in (55.8cm) strips, for the side and base gussets.
Cut 2: 14½in (37.6cm) squares, for sides.

Woven fusible interfacing
Cut 1: 2½in (6.4cm) strip across the width, then cut 1: 34½in (89.6cm) length, for the strap.
Cut 2: 2½in (6.4cm) strips across the width, then cut 2: 21½in (55.8cm) strips, for the side and base gussets.
Cut 2: 14½in (37.6cm) squares, for the sides.

CUTTING GUIDE

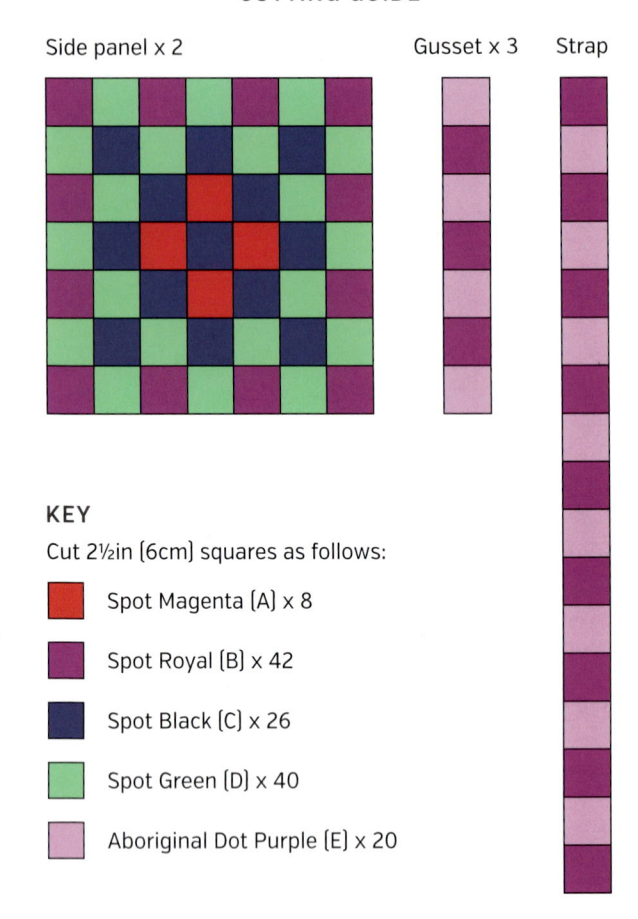

Side panel x 2   Gusset x 3   Strap

KEY
Cut 2½in (6cm) squares as follows:

- Spot Magenta (A) x 8
- Spot Royal (B) x 42
- Spot Black (C) x 26
- Spot Green (D) x 40
- Aboriginal Dot Purple (E) x 20

Alternative strap
A contrasting ribbon is appliquéd to the gussets of the bag and the strap, but you could, if you wished, simply dispense with the patched gusset and strap, and use a wide, thick ribbon in their place.

SEWING THE PATCHWORK PANELS

Use a ¼in (6mm) seam allowance, unless otherwise stated. Both the front and back are made the same way.

1 Lay out all the squares as shown in the photograph.
You need 4 in fabric A; 12 in fabric B; 13 in fabric C; 20 in fabric D, for each side.

2 With RS together and following the instructions on page 117 for sewing blocks, join each vertical row of squares into strips (**A**). Press open seams.

3 Following the instructions on page 117 for crossed seams, join the strips RS together, carefully matching the crossed seams (**B**).

4 Repeat Steps 1 to 3 to make the back piece. When the two patchwork pieces are complete, press open the seams.

A. Joining the squares into strips.

B. Joining the strips to make the patchwork panel.

CHECKERBOARD TOTE BAG 71

MAKING THE STRAP AND GUSSET

These bag elements are lined and interlined for strength.

5 Fuse the interfacing to the corresponding pieces of lining, on the wrong side of the fabric.

Strap

6 To make the strap, alternate 9 fabric B squares with 8 fabric E squares (see diagram on page 70). Stitch together as in Step 2. Press open the seams.

7 Place the lining on top of the pieced strap, RS together. Stitch each long side. Finger press the seam open and turn through to the RS (C). Press.

Gussets

There are three gusset sections (two sides, one base) all constructed in the same way.

8 Lay out the squares in the correct order (see diagram on page 70), using 4 fabric E squares and 3 fabric B squares (D) for each section, and sew them together as in Step 2. Press open the seams.

9 Join the three gussets together into one long strip, positioning them with two fabric E squares at each join. When sewing, start ¼in (6mm) from the edge of the seam and stop ¼in (6mm) short at the end. This will make it easier to turn a corner when sewing to the main panels.

Joining the gusset to the side panels

10 Pin the gussets to the front panel (E), carefully matching the crossed seams (see page 117). Fold excess fabric out of the way at the corners. The corner seam on the gusset should part to make it easier to fit the gusset around the bag. Begin and end the stitching on each of the three seams with a reverse stitch at each corner. Attach the back panel in the same way to the other edge of the gusset strip.

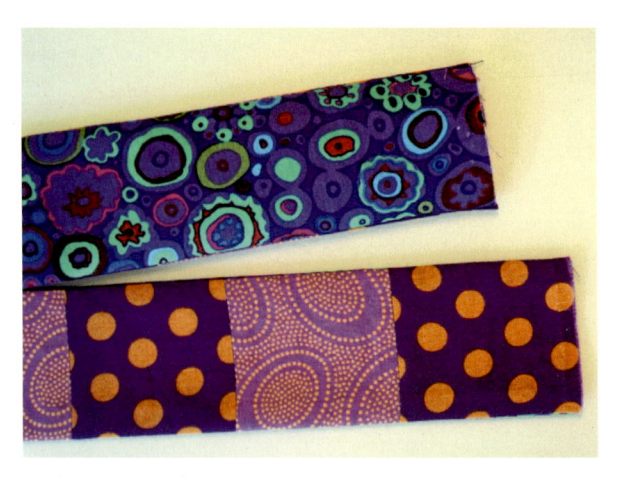

C. The completed strap.

D. Sewing the gusset strip.

E. Pinning the gusset to the front panel.

Attaching the strap

11 Position the strap on the side gusset with the RS together and raw edges aligned, taking care not to twist the strap when you position the other end. Pin the end of the strap horizontally and vertically to prevent it from moving as you sew. Sew in place across the width of the strap (F).

Adding the ribbon

12 If you'd like to add ribbon embellishment, unpick a little opening between two of the squares on the base of the gusset. Pin the ribbon along the center of the gusset and continue along the strap, then the other gusset until you get back to the beginning. Push the ends of the ribbon through the small hole (G).

13 Topstitch (see page 118) in place close to the edge of the ribbon (H). Stitch in the same direction on both sides to prevent the ribbon from twisting. Turn through to the WS and re-stitch the seam to close the small hole.

F. Sewing the strap in place.

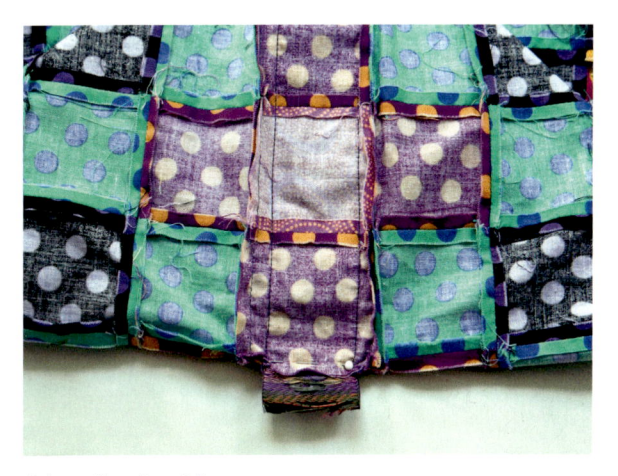

G. Inserting the ribbon.

H. Topstitching the ribbon in place.

CHECKERBOARD TOTE BAG

LINING

The gusset lining is made from two pieces, joined in the center to reduce the bulk at the corners.

14 Make the lining by piecing the gusset lining first, then attaching the two side pieces as in step 10. On the lower edge, on one side of the gusset leave an opening to turn the bag through. Stitch across this opening (I) with a large stitch (see page 118). Finger press the seams open and then remove the large stitches only. Turn RS out.

15 Place the lining inside the outer bag, with RS together, making sure that the handle is inside between the inner and outer layers of the bag (J). Pin and stitch both sides of the front and back panels, leaving the strap unstitched. Turn the bag through the opening in the lining to the RS, push the lining inside the bag, and press.

16 Slip stitch or ladder stitch (see page 118) the gap in the lining closed and slip stitch the lining to the strap on both sides of the bag.

I. Sewing the lining piece.

J. Inserting the lining into the bag outer, RS together.

ADDING A BASE

If you like, you can reinforce the base of the bag with a fabric-covered piece of sturdy card.

17 Cut a 2 x 14in (5.2 x 36.4cm) piece of stiff card. Cut a piece of Paperweight fabric 5½ x 14½in (11.6 x 37.6cm). Fold the fabric along the length with RS together. Stitch along one long side and one short side. Turn through and slide the cardboard inside. Fold under the open end and slip stitch or ladder stitch in place (K). Insert into the base of the bag.

K. Slip stitching the end of the base.

KAFFE FASSETT'S BRILLIANT LITTLE PATCHWORKS

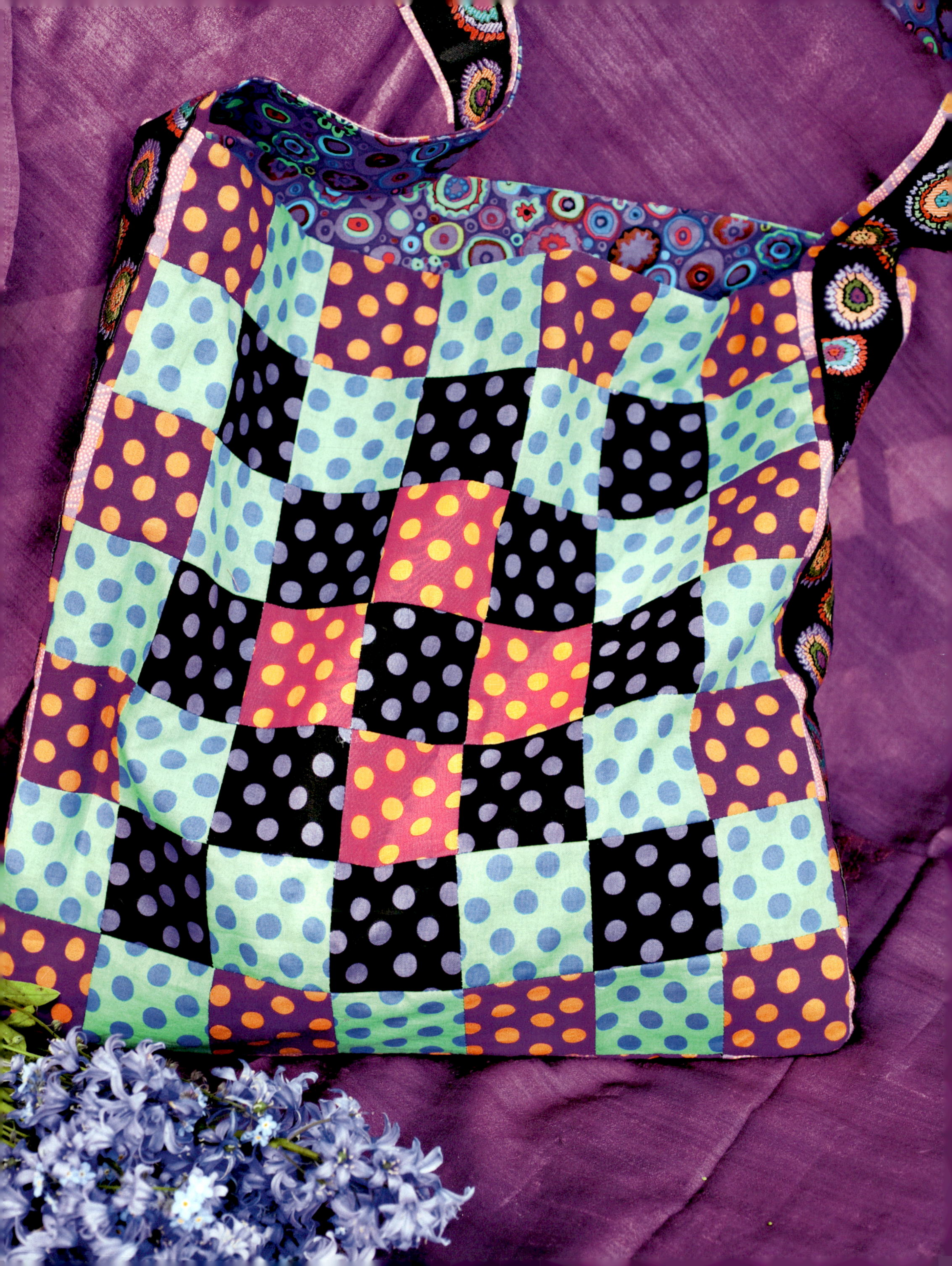

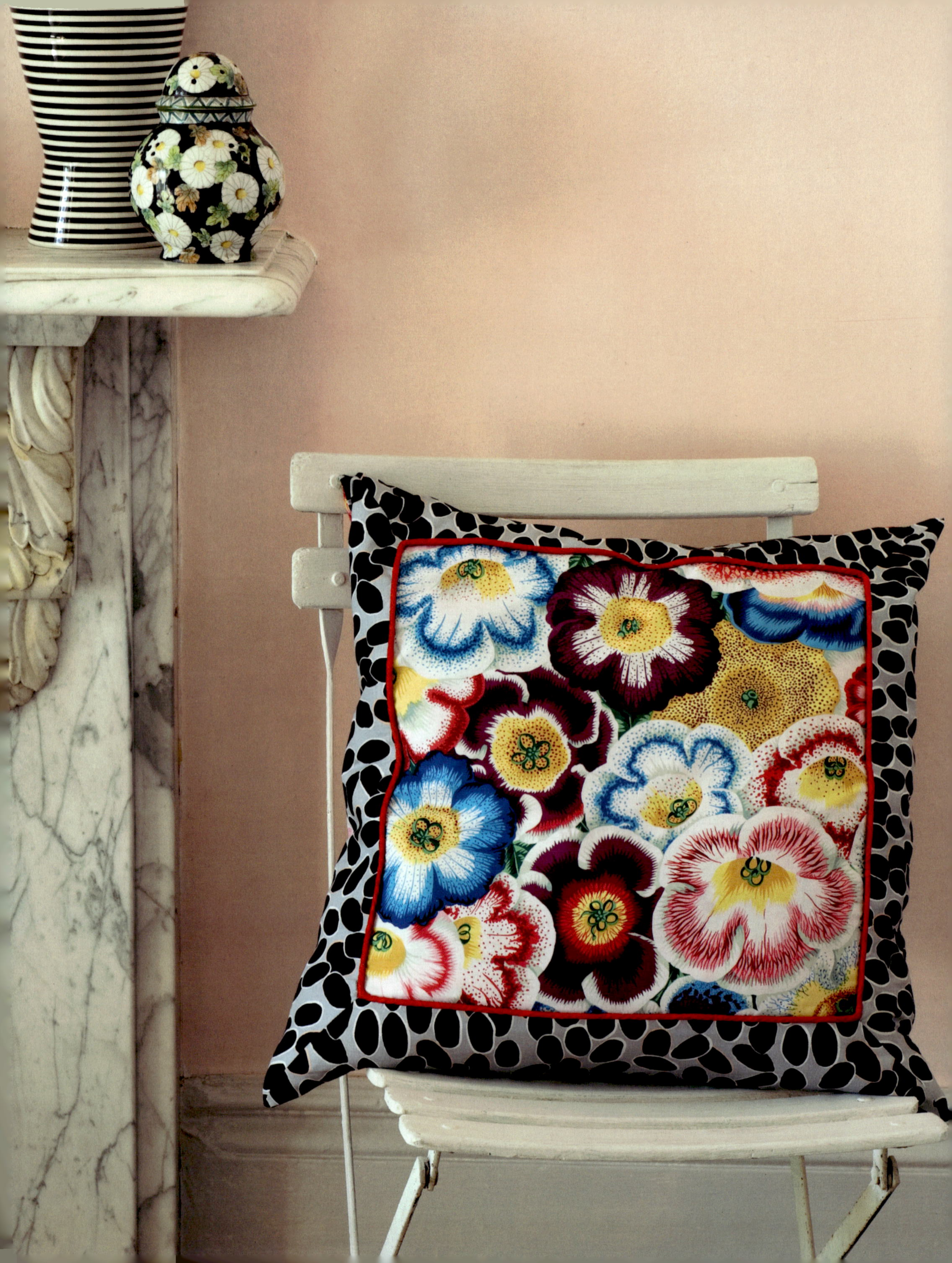

japanese flower cushion

I love the combination of the big dark flowers of my Gloxinias fabric with the black and gray Labels print border, divided by the sharp red piping! The piping fabric was also used for the self-cover buttons on the back of the cushion.

MATERIALS

Gloxinias	Natural	⅝yd (60cm)
Labels	Black	½yd (45cm)
Aboriginal Dot	Red	½yd (45cm)

Other materials

1⅝yd (1.5m) piping cord
Matching cotton thread
5 x 1¼in (3cm) self-cover buttons
20in (51cm) cushion insert

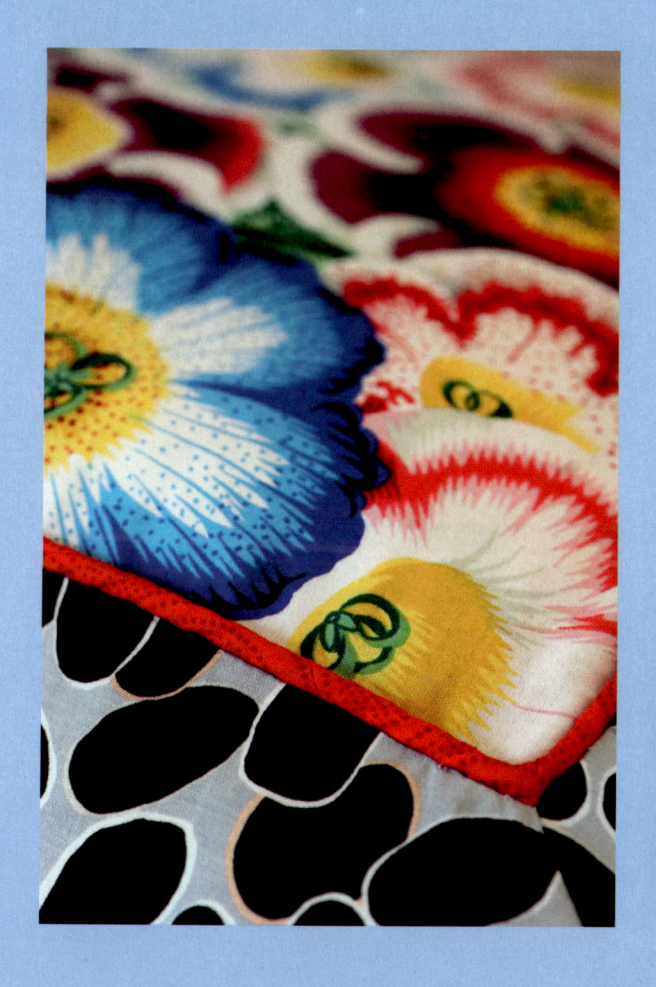

making the japanese flower cushion

FINISHED CUSHION SIZE
Approx. 20 x 20in (51 x 51cm)

CUTTING OUT THE FABRIC
All measurements include a ⅝in (1.5cm) seam allowance.

Front
From Gloxinias Natural, fussy cut (see page 116) 1: 15¼ x 15¼in (38 x 38cm) square for central panel (think about pattern placement and the position of flowers on the front panel).

From Labels Black, cut 4: 23 x 4¼in (58.6 x 10.5cm) rectangles for borders. To miter the borders, trim off the ends at a 45-degree angle. Be very accurate!

From Aboriginal Dot Red, cut enough bias strips to make a ⅝yd (1.5m) length of binding, see page 119.

Back
From Gloxinias Natural, cut 2: 21¼ x 13⅝in (54 x 34.5cm) rectangles.

SEWING THE CUSHION FRONT

Use a ⅝in (1.5cm) seam allowance throughout, unless otherwise stated.

Attaching the piping

1 Follow the instructions on page 119 to make a length of covered piping cord from the Aboriginal Dot Red binding.

2 Begin to pin the covered piping cord to the RS of the central panel, at the lower edge. The raw edges should be aligned and the piping cord facing inward. At each corner snip up to the stitching line on the cord to allow the fabric to turn the corner freely (A).

3 When you get back to the start, cut the piping so that it overlaps the first end by 1in (2.5cm). Remove enough cord from one end, so that the two cord ends meet. Turn under the end of the binding without the cord and wrap over the first end (B). Pin in place.

4 Using an adjustable zipper foot, stitch close to but not tight to the piping cord (C). At each corner, stitch as close as you can. You will have to turn the corner, so lower the needle and raise the presser foot to turn your work.

A. Pinning the covered piping in place.

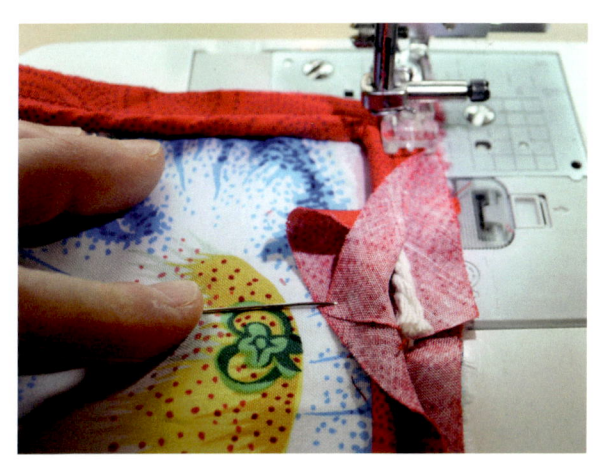

B. Finishing the ends of the piping cord.

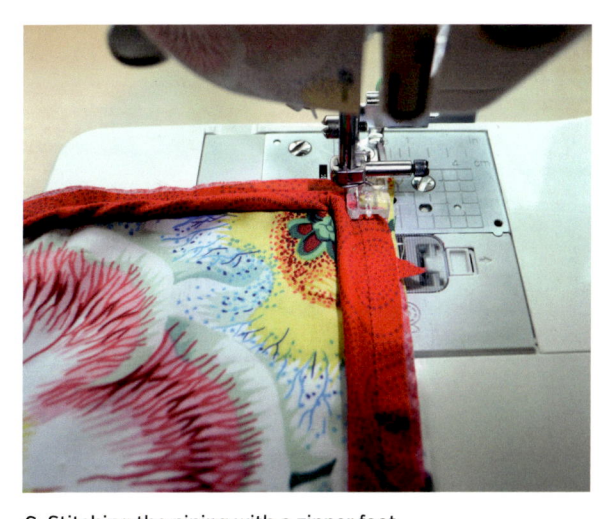

C. Stitching the piping with a zipper foot.

Ringing the color changes

Bright red Aboriginal Dot is used for the piping, but you could easily choose to highlight one of the other colors in the floral print—a yellow, blue, or plum for example, if that fits your decor better—and use up your stash of small print or plain fabrics for the purpose.

JAPANESE FLOWER CUSHION

Sewing the borders

The borders are stitched separately from the central panel and then attached as one piece.

5 Place two border pieces RS together and matching raw edges. Mark ⅝in (1.5cm) from each angled edge, where the seams will converge when joined to the center (**D**).

6 Starting and finishing at the marks, stitch the seam, making sure that you reverse stitch at each end of the seam (**E**).

7 Repeat Steps 6 and 7 with the other three corners to join the remaining borders. Press open all four seams (**F**).

D. Marking the point where the seams converge.

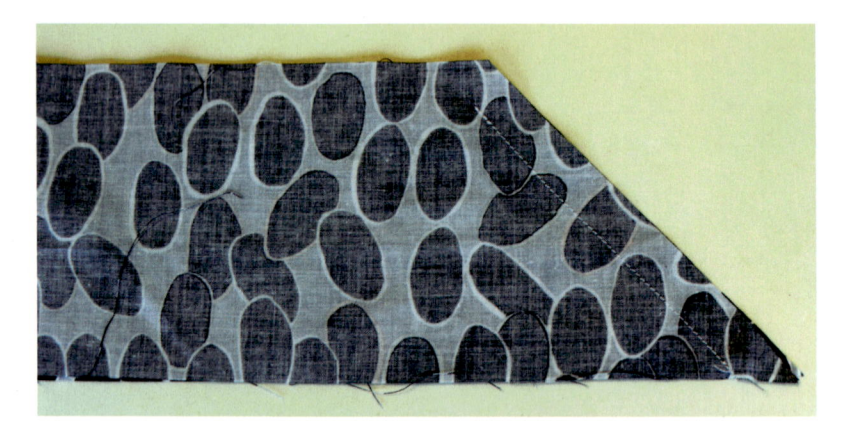

E. Stitching the angled edge.

F. The completed angled seam.

Attaching the border to the central panel

8 Pin the border piece in position on the central panel with RS facing, matching the raw edges, and pinning close to the piping cord and avoiding gaps at the corners (G).

9 Adjust the zipper foot so you can get a little closer to the piping cord and stitch all the way around. Take care when turning the corners—keep them tight and neat, without gaps.

G. Pinning the border to the central panel.

JOINING THE BACK AND FRONT

The cushion has a buttonhole back, but you could make a simple envelope back (see page 120) if you prefer.

10 Follow the instructions on page 120 for making a buttoned cushion back. Stitch the front and back together (H). Trim the corners to remove the bulk, neaten the raw edges, and turn through to the RS.

H. Making the envelope back.

ADDING BUTTONS

11 Follow the instructions on page 120 for making a cushion back with buttons, with five buttonholes. Press. Cover five self-cover buttons with Aboriginal Dot Red (see page 120). Mark the position of the buttons through the center of each buttonhole and sew in place (I).

I. Attaching the buttons.

JAPANESE FLOWER CUSHION

cubist stool cover

I like the very cool, laid back charm of this cover for a simple stool—a cube of chipboard with a foam top. The top and four sides are all the same; a central square combined with two borders—a narrow one in finer striped fabric, and a wider one in broad stripes—all in cool greens and blues. You could switch up the color changes for this, as I have done with the Stripes cushions (see page 21).

MATERIALS

Millefiore	Jade	½yd (45cm)
Caterpillar Stripe	Aqua	⅜yd (35cm)
Narrow stripe	Spring	⅞yd (80cm)

Batting
½yd (45cm)

Other materials
Matching cotton thread

83

making the cubist stool cover

FINISHED COVER SIZE
Approx. 14½ x 14½in (37 x 37cm) square

CUTTING OUT THE FABRIC
All measurements include a ¼in (6mm) seam allowance.

Panels
The cube is made from 5 identical panels.
From Millefiore Jade, fussy cut 5: 6½in (16.5cm) squares.
From Caterpillar Stripe Aqua, cut 4: 2in (4.7cm) strips across the width of the fabric. Then cut 20: 8½in (21.2cm) lengths.
From Narrow Stripe Spring, cut 9: 3in (7.7cm) strips across the width of the fabric. Then cut 20: 12½in (31.2cm) lengths, and cut 4: 15in (38.2cm) lengths for the hem facing.

Lining
From batting, cut 5: 15in (38.2cm) squares.

CUTTING GUIDE

KEY
- Millefiore Jade
- Caterpillar Stripe Aqua
- Narrow Stripe Spring

SEWING THE STOOL COVER

Use a ¼in (6mm) seam allowance throughout, unless otherwise stated. Each of the 5 panels is sewn in the same way. Make 5 panels.

ATTACHING THE INNER BORDER

1 Attach the Caterpillar Stripe border first. With RS facing, position the Millefiore square, 1¾in (4.1cm) down from the short edge of the top border, with a square of border fabric protruding at the right-hand end (A). Begin stitching ¼in (6mm) from the corner of the square.

2 Press all seams open as you work. Position the next border on the left-hand edge (where the first border is flush with the center square) and attach in the same way (B).

3 Repeat to attach the remaining border strips in the same way (C). The protruding part of the first border is stitched to the short end of the fourth border.

A. Attaching the first border to the central panel.

B. Positioning the second border.

C. The completed borders.

Flowers and stripes

Contrasts of floral and geometric prints look good when the color palette of each is closely matched. The cool blue/green tones used here with the Millefiore and the two different striped fabrics could easily be swapped for hot red and orange colorways in the same fabrics.

CUBIST STOOL COVER

ATTACHING THE OUTER BORDER

4 Attach the Narrow Stripe border in the same way as the inner border, but place the first strip of the Narrow Stripe border 2¾in (7.1cm) from the short edge of the Caterpillar border. Complete border as before (D). Press seams open and press the panel. Repeat Steps 1–4 for the remaining panels.

D. The completed Narrow Stripe borders in place.

JOINING THE SIDE PANELS

5 Place each panel RS up on a square of batting and smooth out (E). Pin and baste together (see page 118).

6 Place two side panels RS facing, pin each side seam, and begin stitching ¼in (6mm) in from the top edge with a reverse stitch to secure the seam. Repeat to add the remaining two panels.

E. Basting the panel to the batting.

Alternative cube

The cube-shaped box in these photographs was a simple chipboard box with a foam top (bought from Ikea), but you could easily create a similar one yourself made entirely of firm foam, which has been cut to size (see Suppliers on page 126). Make sure the cube is about ½in (1.2cm) smaller all around than the finished cover size.

86 KAFFE FASSETT'S BRILLIANT LITTLE PATCHWORKS

JOINING THE TOP TO THE SIDES

7 Mark ¼in (6mm) on each corner of the batting on the top panel. Pin the top panel to the cube, matching the mark to the beginning of the side seams (**F**). Stitch in place.

8 Trim away the excess batting (**G**) and press open the seams. Turn the cube right side out.

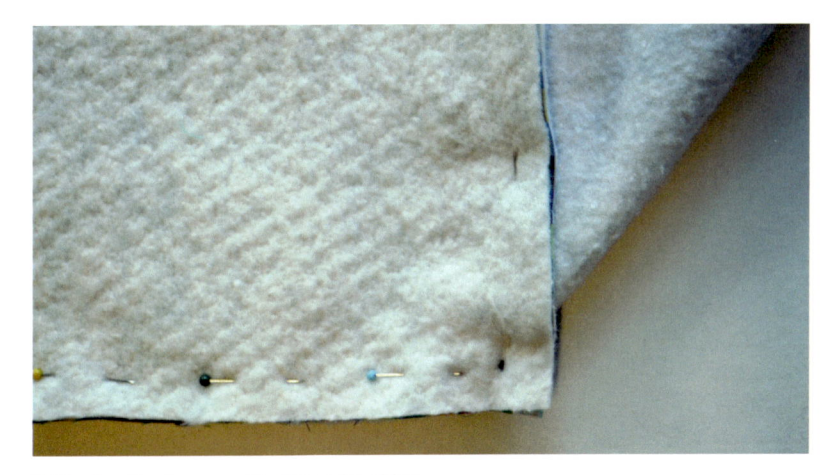

F. Pinning the top panel to the cube sides.

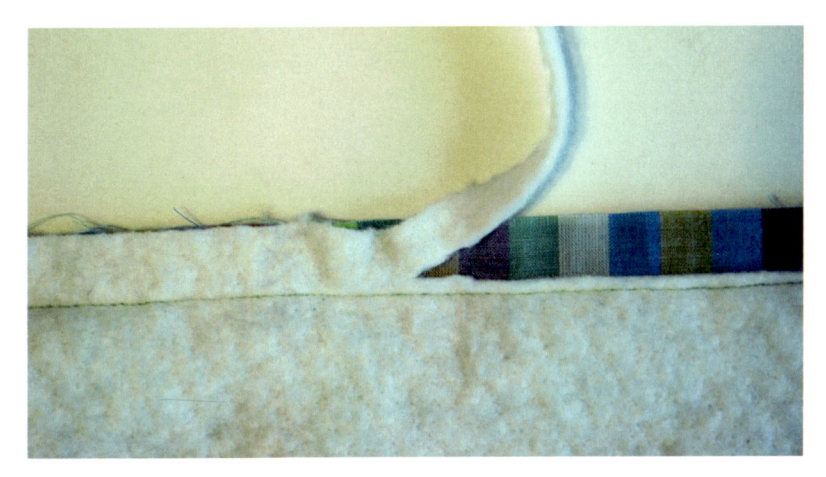

G. Trimming the batting seam allowance.

FINISHING THE HEM

9 Sew the four facing strips together to make one length. Press open the seams and place RS together on the lower edge of the cover. Pin the corner seams so they line up accurately. Stitch in place (**H**).

10 Turn the lower raw edge of the hem under by ¼in (6mm) and slip stitch (see page 118) in place.

H. Adding the facing strip to the base.

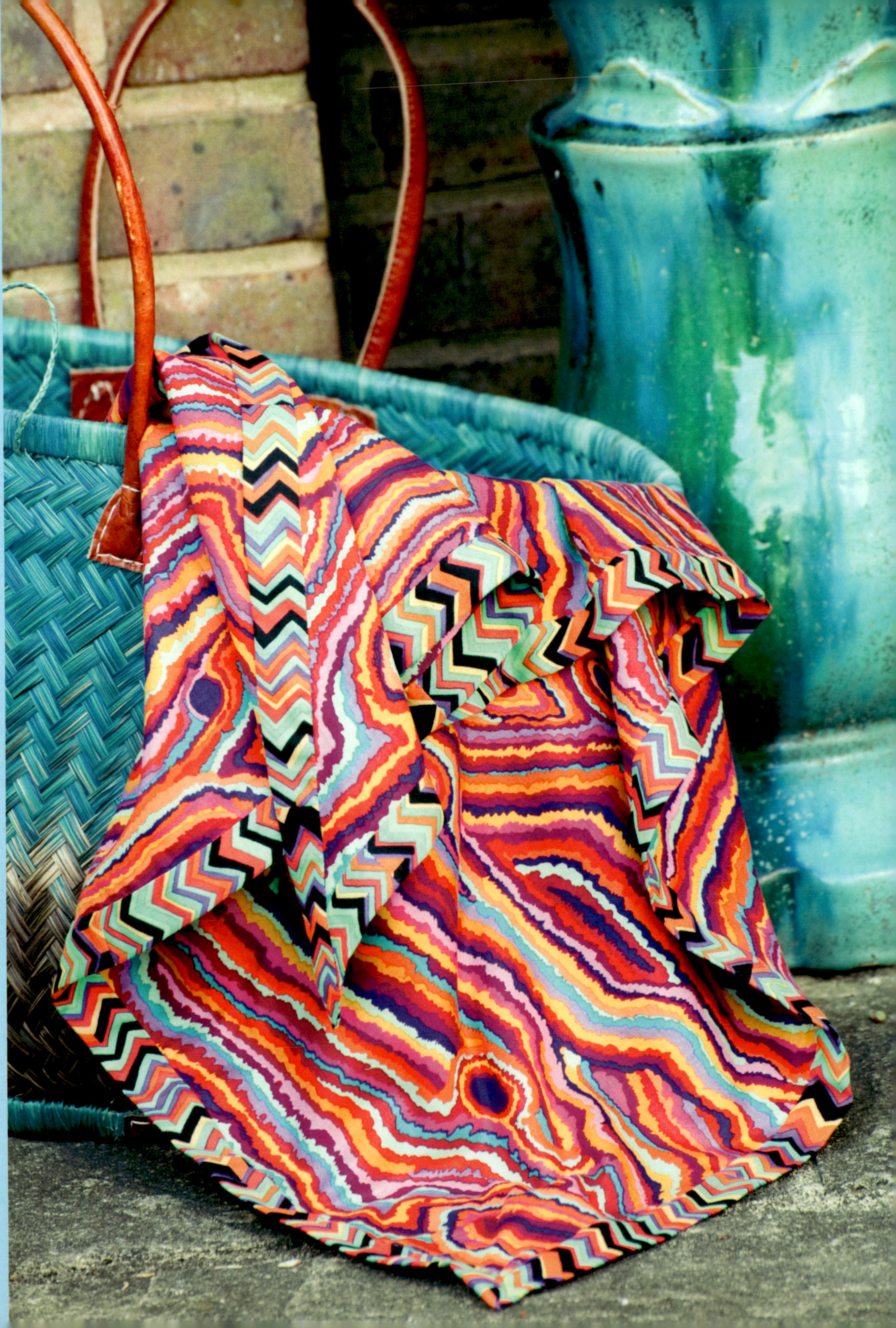

gipsy shawl

This gipsy-style triangular shawl is created very simply from two eye-catching, brilliantly colored contrasting fabrics—Jupiter for the main fabric and Zig Zag for the border. You can wear it as a shawl or tie it, gipsy style, around a plain skirt.

MATERIALS

Jupiter	Red	1¼yd (1.15m)

Binding

Zig Zag	Jade	½yd (45cm)

Other materials
Matching cotton thread

making the gipsy shawl

FINISHED SHAWL SIZE
Long side: 61¼in (156cm)
Shorter sides: 43¼in (110cm)

CUTTING OUT THE FABRIC
From Jupiter, trim the edge of the fabric so that the straight grain is completely straight and is an exact right angle to the selvedge. Remove the selvedges. With the WS facing, fold one corner over to meet the width of the fabric to create a 45-degree angle on the fold. Crease the fold. Trim the remaining edge. Press the diagonal fold on the crease.

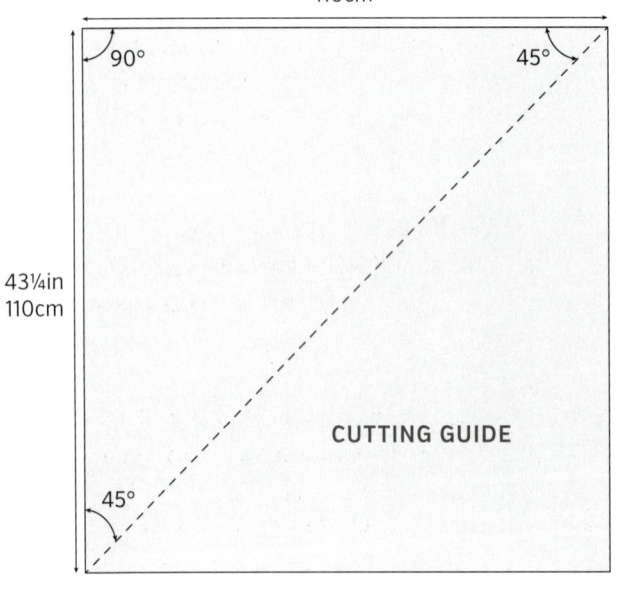

43¼in
110cm

90°   45°

43¼in
110cm

CUTTING GUIDE

45°

Binding
From Zig Zag, cut 10: 2in (5.2cm) strips along the length of the fabric.
To make the binding, sew all the strips together to make a continuous length (see page 119), press open the seams and use a bias binding maker to turn in the raw edges by ¼in (6mm); this small seam allowance will reduce the bulk at the corners.

90   KAFFE FASSETT'S BRILLIANT LITTLE PATCHWORKS

A. Finding the point of the miter.

B. Positioning the binding on the second side.

C. Pinning the binding to the second side.

D. Folding and pinning the final corner.

BINDING THE SHAWL

1 Pin the two layers of fabric together with WS facing. Baste around the edges. Following the instructions on page 119 for binding edges, starting on the long edge, open the binding out and fold the end over by ½in (1.2cm). Position the end of the binding at the tip of the shawl, place the seam allowance of the binding ¾in (2cm) from the raw edge of the shawl. Pin and stitch along the first side on the crease of the binding.

2 Press the binding to fold once more at the crease and with the WS facing, fold the binding over the end, so that the center fold of the binding is aligned to the raw edge of the shawl on the first short side. Place a pin at the point of the fold to determine the point of miter (**A**). This should line up with the fold on the long edge of the shawl.

3 Crease the end of the binding and remove the pin. Turn the shawl over so the binding is RS facing upward. The center fold of the binding should lie on top of the raw edge (**B**). Pin in place, right on the very edge of the binding, for 2–3in (5–7cm).

4 Continue to pin the binding ¾in (2cm) from the raw edge of the shawl (**C**) and stitch in place. Continue binding the third side (see page 119 for binding a mitered right-angle corner).

5 Fold the binding to the back of the shawl, over the stitched edges, and pin in place. Fold the miters on the first two corners to match the angle of the shawl. You may have to tuck in a little extra fabric on the 45 degree corner (**D**). On the last corner where the binding ends meet, fold under the raw edges to the shape of the corner, trimming any excess fabric. Pin in place.

Finishing the binding

6 On the reverse side of the shawl, slip stitch in place. Try to keep the corners as neat as possible, and slip stitch each corner as you reach it.

GIPSY SHAWL

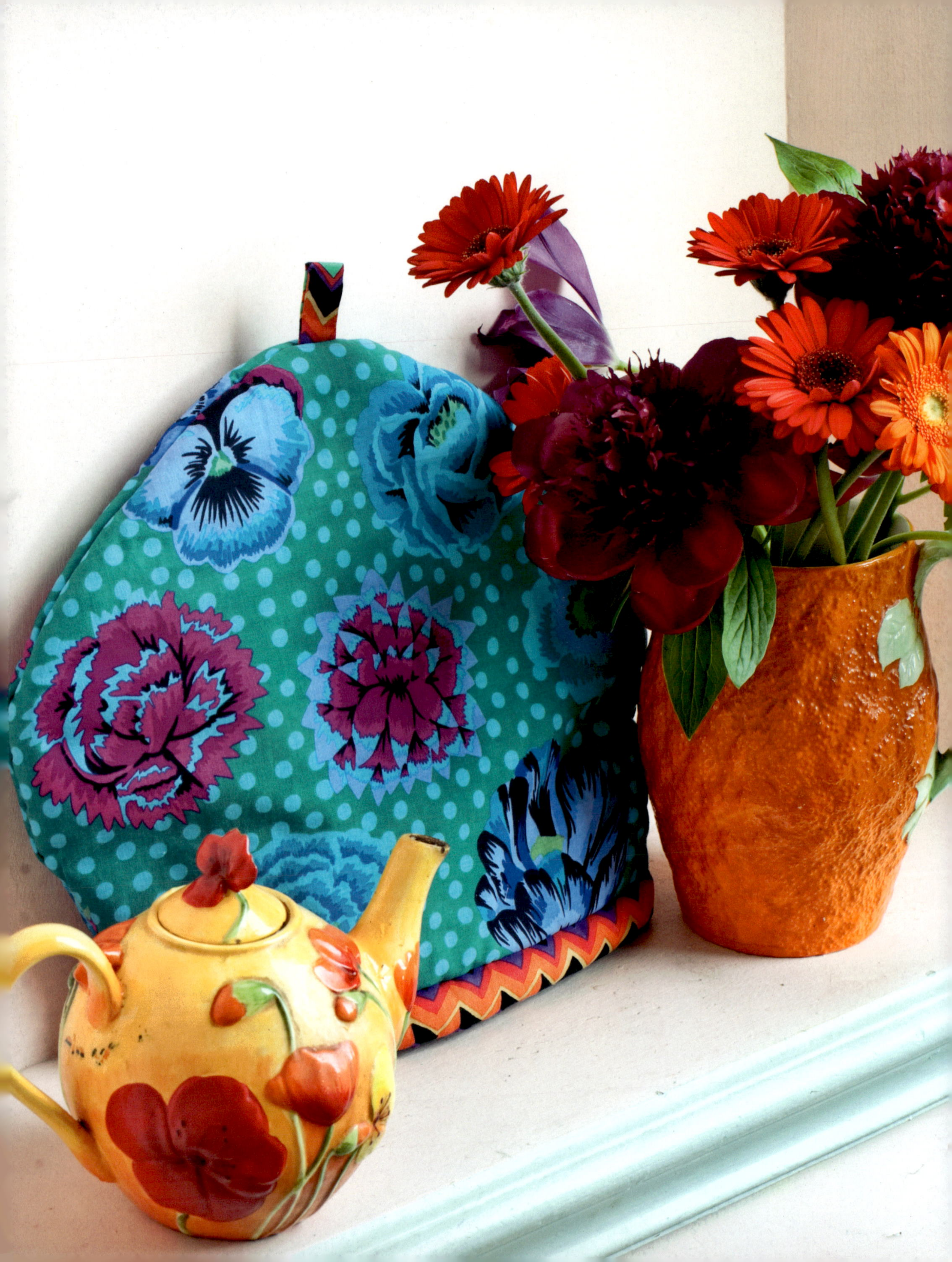

big tea cozy

This tea cozy is big enough to fit most teapots, but it is always wise to measure yours first! The main fabric is the striking Big Blooms, edged with Zig Zag and lined with Jupiter (and also interlined with batting to keep in the heat).

MATERIALS
Big Blooms   Emerald   ½yd (45cm)

Lining
Jupiter   Malachite   ½yd (45cm)

Binding
Zig Zag   Jade   ½yd (45cm)

Other materials
Pattern paper
Matching cotton thread
2oz (75g) polyester batting   ½yd (45cm)

making the big tea cozy

FINISHED COZY SIZE
Height: 12½in (32cm)
Width: 14½in (36.5cm)

PREPARATION
Enlarge Template D on page 123 by 200% and cut out.

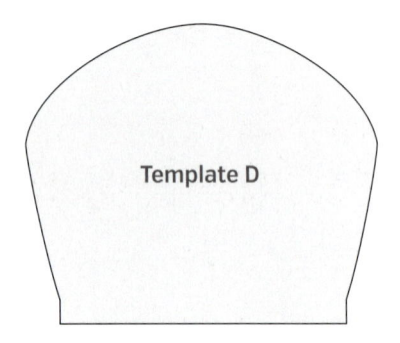

Template D

CUTTING THE FABRIC
All measurements include a ⅝in (1.5cm) seam allowance.

Outer
From Big Blooms, cut 2: main panels. Think about the pattern placement and where the flowers sit within the shape of the pattern.

Lining
From Jupiter Malachite, cut 2: main panels.

Binding
From Zig Zag Jade, cut 1: 3¼in (8cm) strip across the width of the fabric.
Fold in half lengthwise and press. Turn the raw edges in to meet the fold and press.

Loop
Cut 1: 3¼in (8cm) length from the binding strip.

Batting
Cut 2: main panels.

SEWING THE TEA COZY
Use a ⅝in (1.5cm) seam allowance throughout, unless otherwise stated.

Preparing the layers

1 Fold the loop strip in half lengthwise with RS together and stitch ¾in (2cm) from the fold along the length. Finger press the seam and turn through to the RS. Press.

2 Fold the loop in half widthwise and position in the center on the top edge of one piece of Big Blooms, with raw edges aligned and the loop facing inward. Stitch in place, within the seam allowance (A).

A. Stitching the loop in place.

Alternative tea cozy top
The loop on top of the tea cozy is not essential, so you could leave it out. Alternatively, you could create a topknot for the cozy made from little strips of brightly colored felt, and stitched in as you would do for the loop.

Joining the layers

3 Layer the fabrics in the following order: place both Big Blooms outer pieces RS together; place one piece of batting on top; place two pieces of Jupiter with RS together on top; and then the second piece of batting (B).

4 Pin around the top, curved edge. Using a walking foot, stitch around the cozy. Trim excess batting and turn through to the RS.

B. Layering the fabrics and batting.

ADDING BINDING

5 Separate the two sides of the cozy with the lining in the middle (outer layer, batting, and lining). Pin and baste the three layers together at the lower edge on each side.

6 Place the binding on the lower edge of the outer cozy with RS together, ½in (1.2cm) before the first side seam. Align the raw edges of the binding and the outer, with the binding facing inward and pin in place (C).

7 Work around the cozy and when you get back to the beginning, cut the binding 1in (2.5cm) longer than you need. Fold the end of the binding under, so that the fold lies along the side seam. Stitch around the lower edge, following the crease in the binding.

8 Turn under the binding to the inside of the cozy and slip stitch or ladder stitch (see page 118) in place (D). For extra padding, you could place a strip of batting inside the binding before you hand stitch it in place.

C. Positioning the binding.

D. The completed binding.

BIG TEA COZY 95

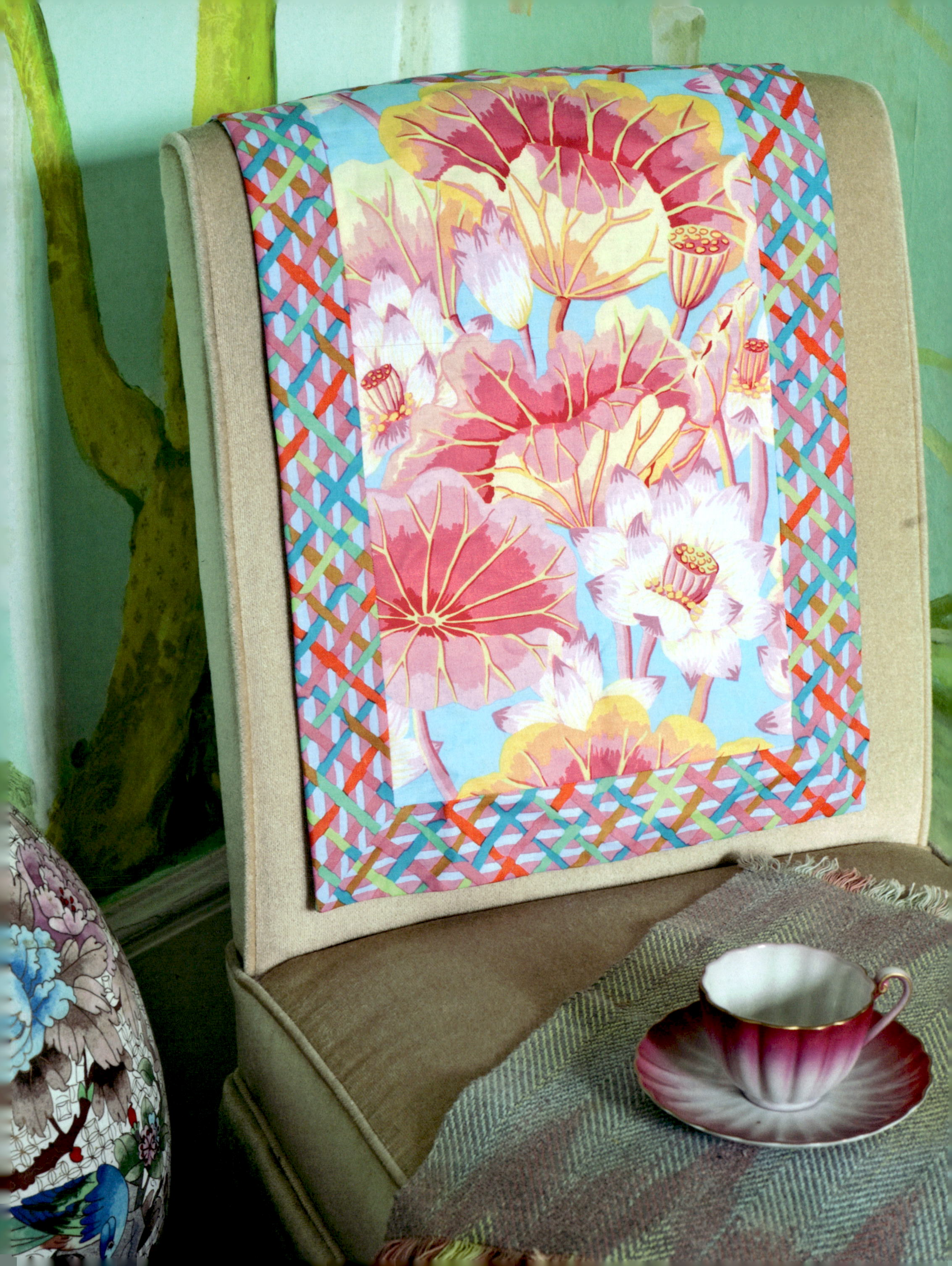

lattice chair back throw

It can be fun to liven up an old or plain chair with a little throw of its own. This one uses a contrast of Lake Blosssoms bordered with Mad Plaid, and lined with Spot. As with quite a few of my projects, I have set off a big floral fabric with a geometric pattern for the border. For this throw I have picked up the colors in the main fabric for the border. Mitered corners need to be worked carefully to get a neat finish.

MATERIALS
Central panel
Lake Blossoms   Pink   ¾yd (70cm)

Borders
Mad Plaid   Candy   ¼yd (25cm)

Backing
Spot   Lavender   ½yd (45cm)

Other materials
Matching cotton thread

making the lattice chair back throw

FINISHED CHAIR BACK SIZE
Approx. 20 x 14in (50.4 x 36cm)

CUTTING THE FABRIC
All measurements include a ¼in (6mm) seam allowance.

Central panel
From Lake Blossoms Pink, cut 1: 16½ x 10½in (41.2 x 26.8cm) rectangle. Think about the pattern placement and where the flowers sit within the rectangle.

Borders
From Mad Plaid Candy, cut 2: 2½in (6.4cm) strips across the width of the fabric.
From these strips, cut 2: 20¾in (52.4cm) strips; cut 2: 14¾in (38cm) strips.
To miter the borders, trim off the ends at a 45-degree angle. Be very accurate!

Backing
From Spot Lavender, cut 1: 20½ x 14½in (51.6 x 37.2cm) rectangle.

SEWING THE CHAIR BACK
Use a ¼in (6mm) seam allowance throughout, unless otherwise stated.

Attaching the borders

1 On the WS of the central panel mark each corner, ¼in (6mm) in from each side.

2 Following the instructions on page 119 for attaching mitered borders, pin the long side borders in position with RS facing (A) and stitch from one corner dot to the next.

3 Attach the top and bottom border in the same way (B), stitching from dot to dot. Press the seams toward the border.

A. Stitching the side borders.

B. Attaching the top border.

Securing the throw
If you want to make sure the throw does not slip on the chair it covers, you could stitch a narrow strip of velcro to the backing fabric near the top edge (similar to the way the heading slot is made on on page 103), which will help to prevent it from sliding down.

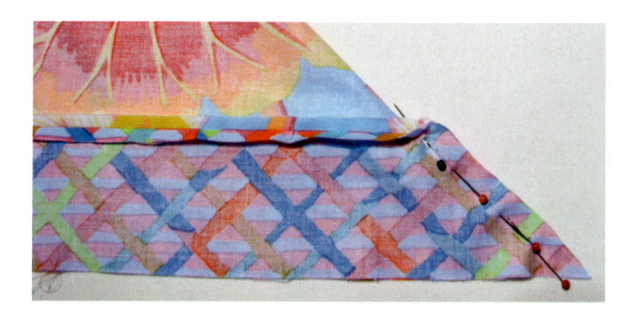

C. Stitching the diagonal seam on the border.

D. Joining the back and front panels, RS together.

E. Pinning the layers together.

F. Slip stitching the opening.

Mitering the borders

4 To join the corner seams on the borders, fold the central panel in half diagonally. Match the raw edges of the border, pin and stitch from the dot to the corner of the border (C). Press the seams open. Repeat to sew the remaining corners.

Joining the front and backing

5 Place the backing and front panel RS together (D).

6 Pin all the way around (E), leaving an opening of 4in (10cm), to turn through. Following the instructions on page 118 for stitching openings, stitch the two layers together.

7 Trim the corners and finger press all the seams. Turn the chair back through to the RS and press. Stitch the opening closed (F) using slip stitch or ladder stitch (see page 118).

LATTICE CHAIR BACK THROW

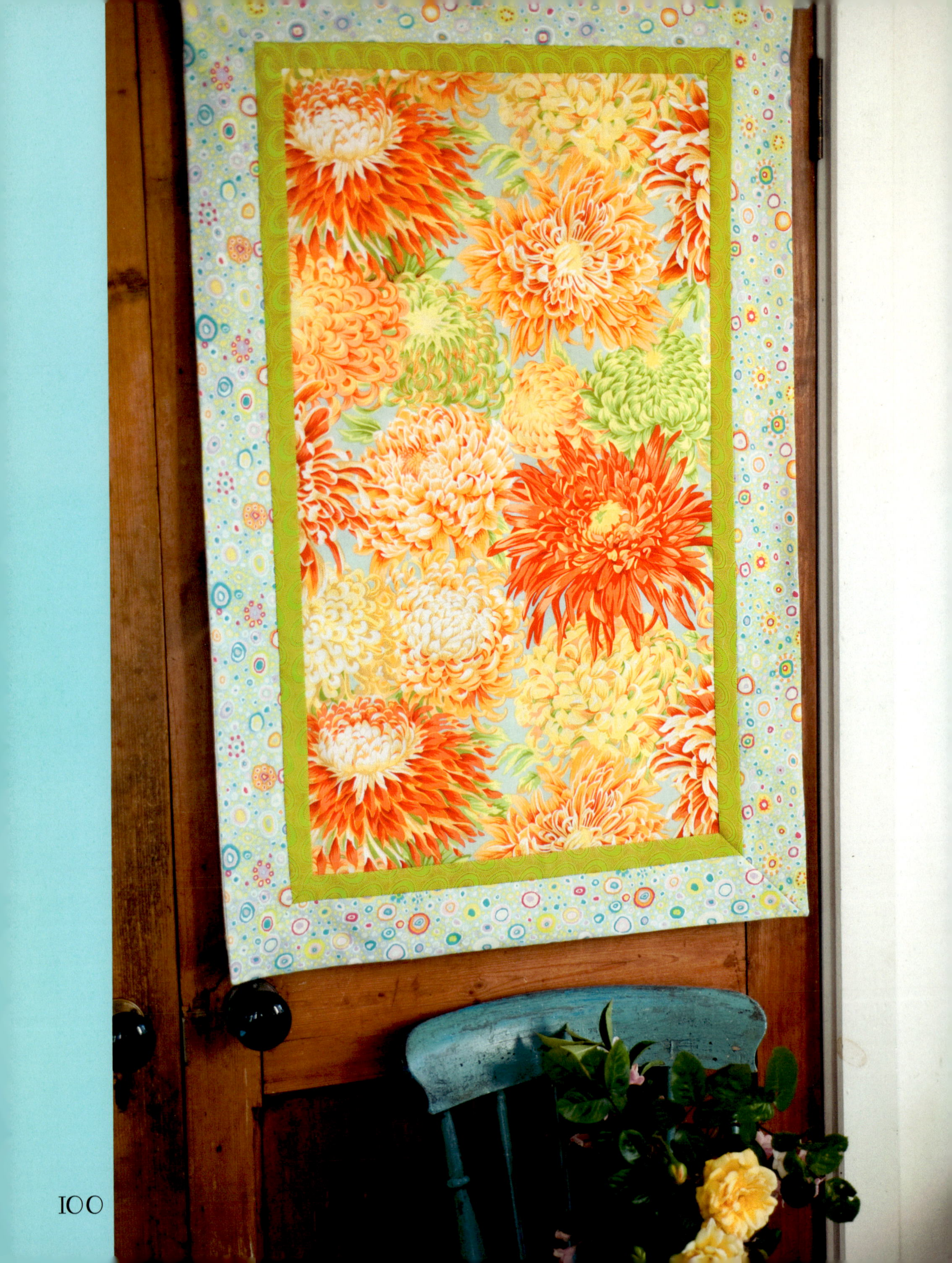

chrysanthemum panel

This simple design will provide a cheerful screen for a glass door. I opted for a big bold fabric for the central panel, and then bordered it with two geometric-style prints for a narrow inner border and a wider outer one. The corners are mitered to give it a sharper finish.

MATERIALS
Central panel

Japanese Chrysanthemum	Yellow	1yd (90cm)
Aboriginal Dot	Lime	⅜yd (35cm)
Roman Glass	Pastel	⅝yd (60cm)

Backing

Aboriginal Dot	Cream	1⅜yd (1.25m)

Woven fusible interfacing
26 x 3in (66 x 7.5cm)

Other materials
Matching cotton thread

CHRYSANTHEMUM PANEL 101

making the chrysanthemum panel

FINISHED PANEL SIZE
Approx. 42 x 27in (105 x 68.5cm)

CUTTING THE FABRIC
All measurements include a ¼in (6mm) seam allowance.

Central panel
From Japanese Chrysanthemum Yellow, cut 1: 31½ x 16½in (78.2 x 41.7cm) rectangle. Think about the pattern placement and where the flowers sit within the rectangle.

Borders
From Aboriginal Dot Lime, cut 2: 2¼in (5.6cm) strips across the width of the fabric.
From these strips, cut 2: 35¾in (88.8cm) strips for the long borders; cut 2: 20¾in (52.3cm) strips for the short borders.
To miter the borders, trim off the ends at a 45-degree angle. Be very accurate!
From Roman Glass Pastel, cut 2: 4¼in (10.8cm) strips across the width of the fabric.
From these strips, cut 2: 43¼in (105cm) strips for the long borders; cut 2: 28¼in (71.5cm) strips for the short borders.
To miter the borders, trim off the ends at a 45-degree angle. Be very accurate!

Backing
From Aboriginal Dot Cream, cut 1: 42½ x 27½in (106.2 x 69.7cm) rectangle.
Cut 1: 26 x 3¼in (66cm x 8cm) rectangle, for slot heading.

Interfacing
Cut 1: 26 x 3in (66 x 7.5cm) strip.

SEWING THE FRONT PANEL
Use a ¼in (6mm) seam allowance throughout, unless otherwise stated.

ATTACHING THE BORDERS

1 On the WS of the central panel mark each corner, ¼in (6mm) in from each side.

2 Following the instructions on page 119 for attaching mitered borders, pin the long side borders in position with RS facing and then stitch from one corner dot to the next.

3 Attach the top and bottom borders in the same way, stitching from dot to dot (A). Press the seams toward the border.

4 Following steps 2 and 3, attach the Roman Glass borders, starting with the long side borders then attaching the short top and bottom borders. Press the seams toward the border.

A. Attaching the top border.

MITERING THE BORDERS

5 To join the corner seams on the borders, fold the central panel in half diagonally. Match the raw edges of the border, aligning the seam joining the two fabrics, pin, and stitch from the dot to the corner of the border. Press the seams open (B). Repeat to sew the remaining corners.

B. Pressing the seams on the completed diagonal seams.

SEWING THE BACKING

Sewing the slot heading

6 Fuse the strip of interfacing to the WS of the backing, centered ⅝in (1.5cm) down from the top edge (C).

7 On the small rectangle of fabric for the slot heading, turn a ¼in (6mm) double hem on each short end and stitch in place. Turn under ⅝in (1.5cm) on each long edge and press.

8 Position the slot heading on the RS of the backing, ¾in (2cm) from the top edge and centered 1in (2.5cm) in from each side. Topstitch (see page 118) in place, making sure to reinforce the stitching at either end on both edges (D).

C. Fusing the interfacing to the backing.

JOINING THE FRONT AND BACKING

9 Place the front and backing with RS together. Pin all the way around, leaving an opening of 4in (10cm) at the top edge, to turn through. Following the instructions on page 118 for stitching openings, stitch the two layers together.

10 Trim the corners, finger press all seams, and remove the large stitches at the opening. Turn the panel through to the RS and press. Slip stitch or ladder stitch the opening (see page 118).

D. Topstitching the slot heading in place.

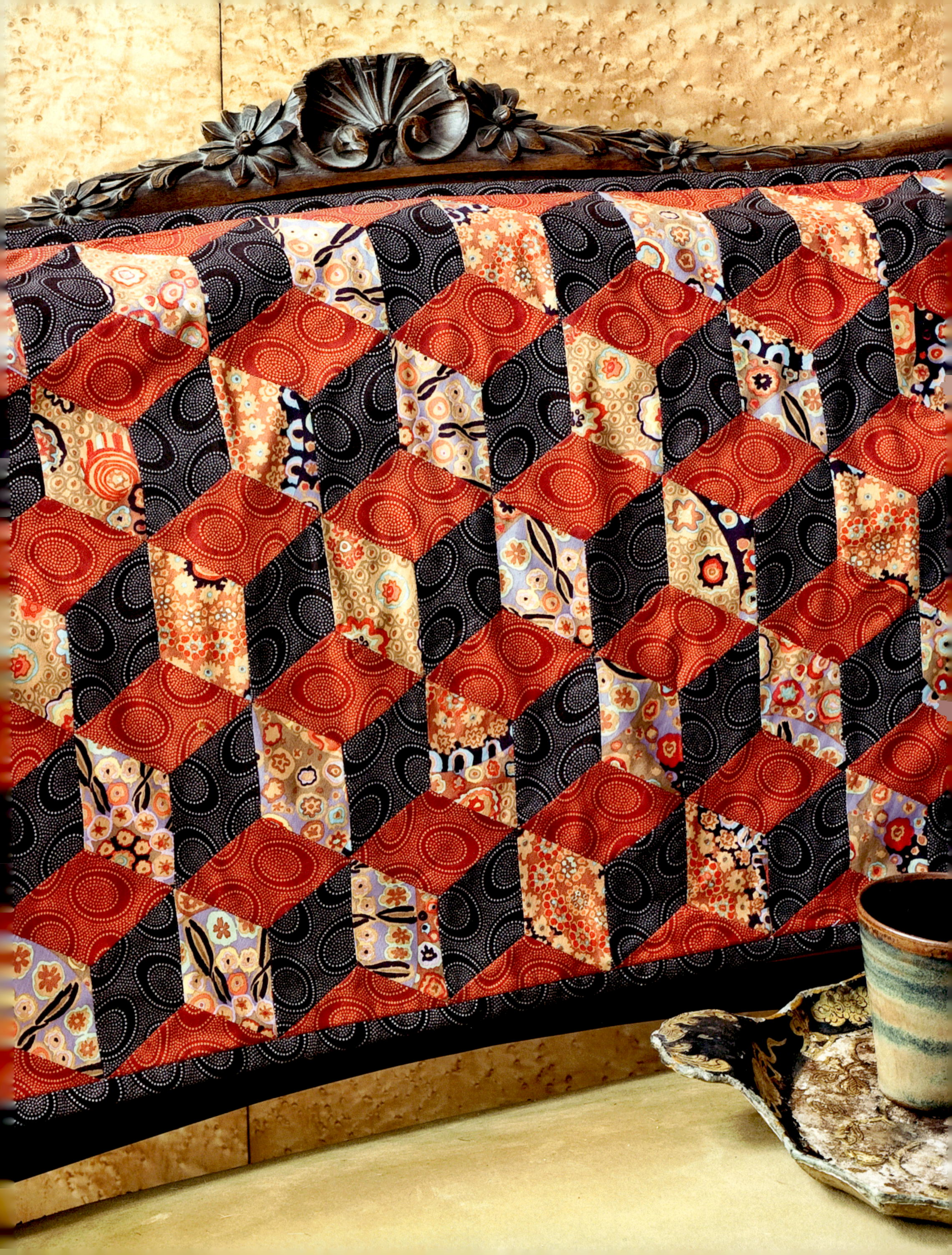

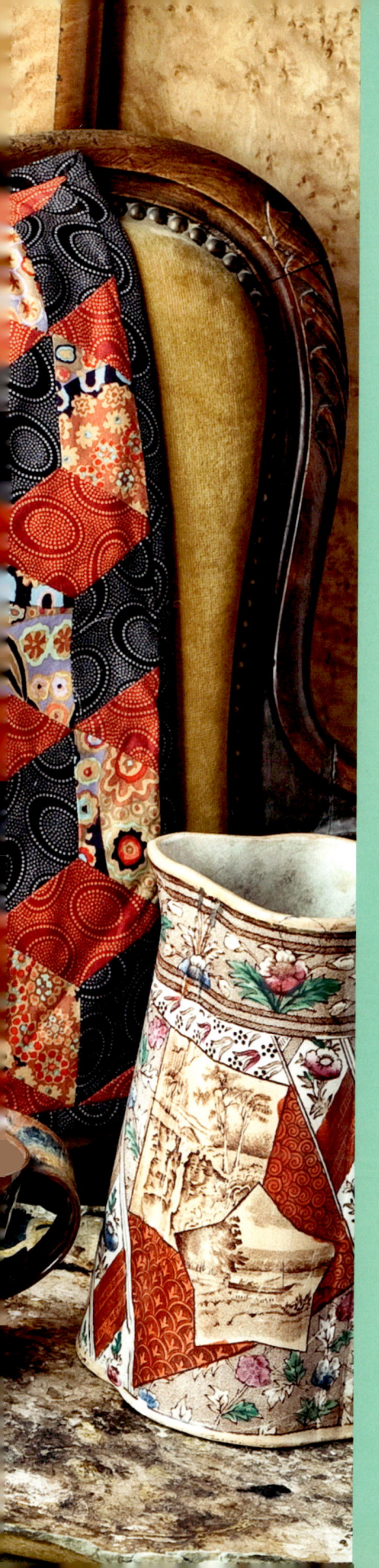

tumbling blocks panel

You can use this little panel to cover the back of a chair. It will work either way up. It comprises a traditional tumbling blocks design, which creates a curious 3-D effect. I used two colors of Aboriginal Dot fabric, combined with Millefiore; a small flower print with occasional flashes of turquoise in the particular colorway chosen.

MATERIALS
Patchwork diamonds

Millefiore	Brown	⅜yd (35cm)
Aboriginal Dot	Chocolate	⅝yd (60cm)
Aboriginal Dot	Pumpkin	⅜yd (35cm)

Backing

Spot	Tobacco	½yd (45cm)

Batting
½yd (45cm)

Other materials
Template plastic
Matching cotton thread

making the tumbling blocks panel

FINISHED PANEL SIZE
Approx. 34 x 18in (85 x 44.5cm)

PREPARATION
Copy Template E on page 123 onto template plastic and cut out. Transfer the marks to the template.

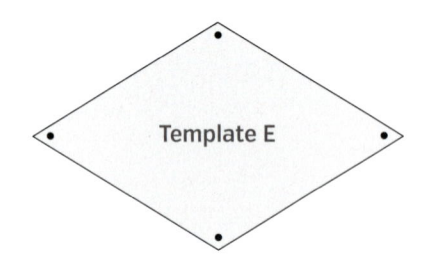

Template E

CUTTING THE FABRIC
All measurements include a ¼in (6mm) seam allowance.

Patchwork
From Millefiore Brown, cut 4: 2⅜in (5.9cm) strips across the width of the fabric.
From three strips, cut 13 diamonds; cut 3 diamonds from the last strip, to give a total of 42 diamonds.

From Aboriginal Dot Chocolate, cut 4: 2⅜in (5.9cm) strips across the width of the fabric.
From three strips, cut 13 diamonds; cut 4 diamonds from the last strip, to give a total of 43 diamonds.

From Aboriginal Dot Pumpkin, cut 4: 2⅜in (5.9cm) strips across the width of the fabric.
From each strip, cut 13 diamonds, to give a total of 52 diamonds.

Binding
From Aboriginal Dot Chocolate, cut 3: 2in (5cm) strips across the width of the fabric. Follow the instructions on page 119 to make a binding strip.

CONSTRUCTING THE PATCHWORK FRONT PANEL

Use a ¼in (6mm) seam allowance throughout, unless otherwise stated.

1 Using the template, transfer the dots on each corner to the back of each fabric diamond, so that you can match each seam (A).

Stitching the first row

2 Pin an Aboriginal Dot Chocolate and Millefiore diamond with RS together. Stitch from dot to dot on one side, making sure that you start and finish the seam with a reverse stitch to secure the seam (B).

3 Add another Aboriginal Dot Chocolate to the opposite side of the Millefiore diamond (C) and keep adding alternating Millefiore and Aboriginal Dot Chocolate diamonds to complete a row of 17 diamonds (9 Aboriginal Dot Chocolate and 8 Millefiore). Repeat Steps 2 and 3 to make 2 more rows. Repeat Steps 2 and 3 twice more, but this time begin and end each row with a Millefiore.

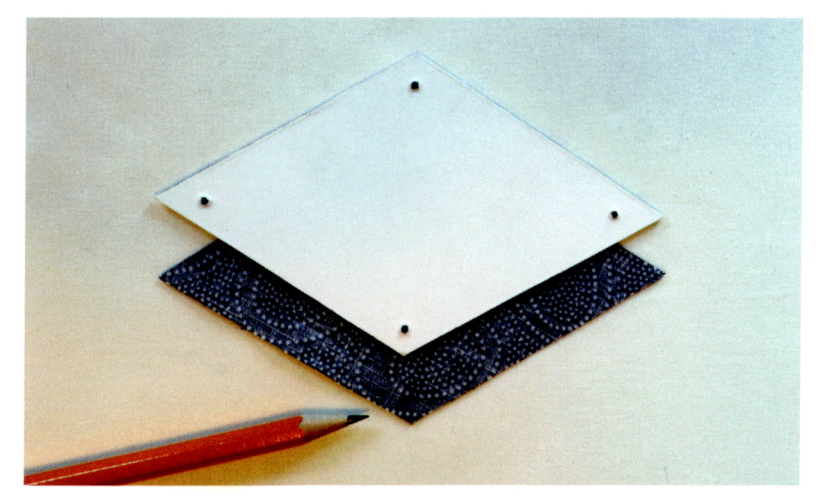

A. Transferring the dots from the template.

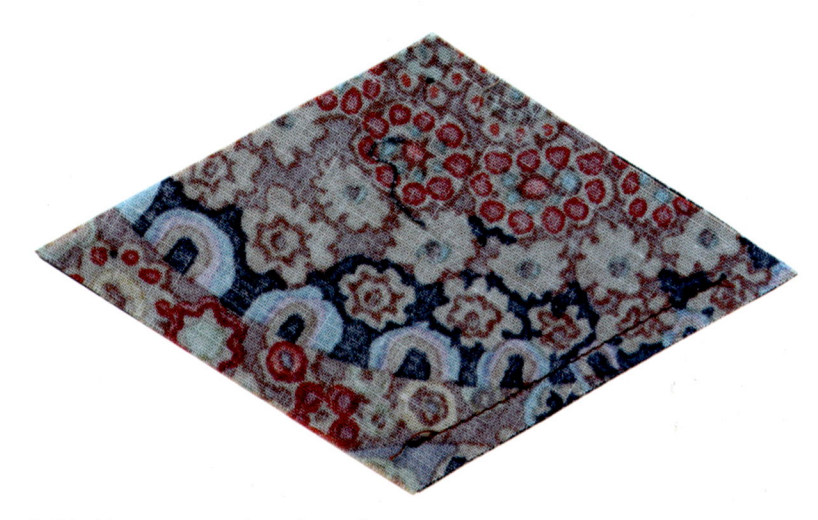

B. Stitching one seam, from dot to dot.

C. Adding the next diamond to the opposite side.

TUMBLING BLOCKS PANEL

Attaching the diamonds

4 Take a row of sewn diamonds beginning and ending with Aboriginal Dot Chocolate. Pin an Aboriginal Dot Pumpkin diamond, RS facing with the first Aboriginal Dot Chocolate and sew together between the dots. Pin the next Aboriginal Dot Pumpkin diamond, RS facing to the Millefiore diamond and sew between the dots (D). Fold the Millefiore diamond across the width and line up the raw edge of the Pumpkin diamond and second Chocolate Aboriginal Dot diamond with RS facing, then stitch between the dots. Continue in this way to complete the tumbling block pattern (E).

5 Join another nine Aboriginal Dots Pumpkin diamonds to the base of the strip. Take a row of sewn diamonds beginning and ending with Millefiore diamonds and sew this to the second row of Pumpkin diamonds, sewing from dot to dot as before to inset the shapes.

6 Attach another row of Aboriginal Dot Pumpkin diamonds, starting from the left-hand edge. Press the seams open as you work.

7 Attach another row of sewn diamonds, this time beginning and ending with Aboriginal Dot Chocolate, and then another Aboriginal Dot Pumpkin row. Continue, alternating the rows, following the assembly diagram (F). Press the panel when complete.

D. Sewing the diamonds together in a strip.

E. Attaching the Aboriginal Dot Pumpkin diamonds to the completed row.

F. Layout for assembling the rows.

G. Trimming the points from the diamonds.

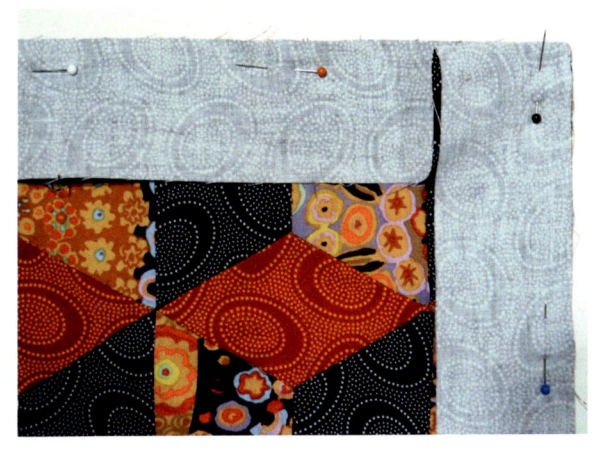

H. Pinning the binding in place.

ADDING THE BACKING AND BINDING

8 Press the panel top. Take the backing fabric and batting and cut to the correct size for the panel, which should be 34 x 18in (85 x 44.5cm). It is worth checking the measurements of your pieced panel top first, bearing in mind that the protruding triangles will be cut off. Place the panel top RS down and layer the batting and the backing on top, RS facing up. Trim the edges to fit the backing, cutting off any protruding diamonds on the short and long edges (G). Baste the layers together (see page 120)

Binding the edges

9 Pin the binding in place (H) and follow the instructions on page 119 for binding edges with mitered corners. Stitch in place (I).

10 Slip stitch or ladder stitch (see page 118) the binding in place on the reverse (J). Remove the basting stitches added in Step 8.

I. Stitching the binding.

J. Slip stitching the binding on the reverse.

TUMBLING BLOCKS PANEL 109

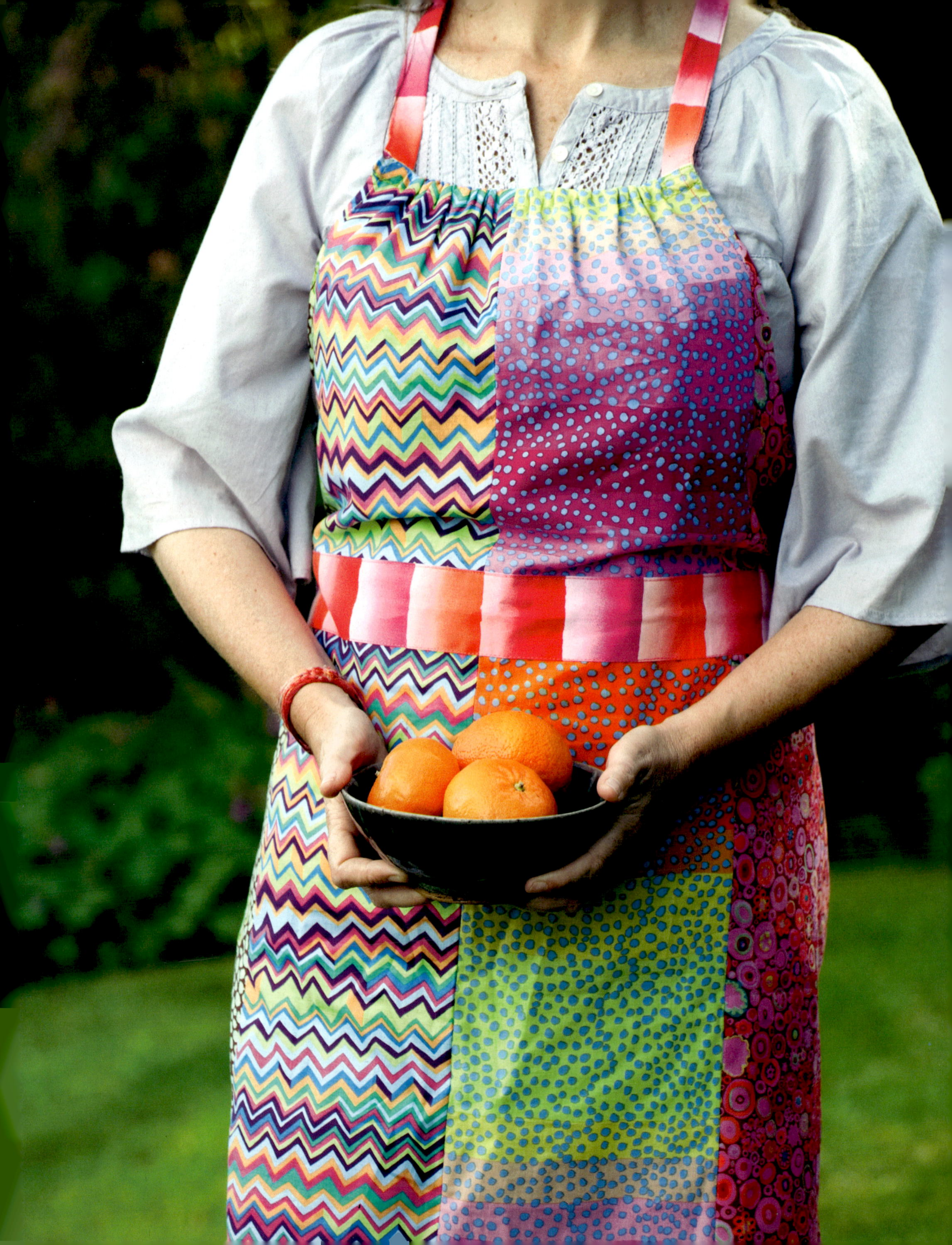

jazz apron

The rich mix of color and pattern in this bib style apron is enhanced by the eye-catching broad stripes of the ribbon used for the waistband and neck ties. A very simple patchwork, it combines small print flowers, spots, and zigzag stripes in a riot of hot colors.

MATERIALS

Guinea Flower	Green	¼yd (25cm)
Zig Zag	Multi	1yd (90cm)
Ombre	Pink	1yd (90cm)
Paperweight	Pink	¼yd (25cm)
Kim	Red	½yd (45cm)

Other materials
Pattern paper
Matching cotton thread
¼yd (23cm) cotton tape, ¼in (6mm) wide

making the jazz apron

FINISHED APRON SIZE
Approx. 31 x 28in (78 x 72cm)

PREPARATION
Make a paper pattern following the diagram. To create the armhole, draw a 3in (7.5cm) vertical line from the top and flatten the curved line as it turns horizontal at the side.

CUTTING THE FABRIC
All measurements include a ⅝in (1.5cm) seam allowance.

Main panels
From Guinea Flower Green, cut 1: side panel across the width, with RS facing. Place the pattern with the armhole on the left.
From Zig Zag Multi, cut 1: central panel from the length of the fabric.
From Ombre Pink, cut 1: central panel from the length of the fabric.
From Paperweight Pink, cut 1: side panel across the width, with RS facing. Place the pattern with the armhole on the right.

Waist ties
From Kim, cut 2: 32 x 5¼in (80 x 13cm) rectangles across the width of the fabric.

Front waistband
From Kim, cut 1: 29½ x 4in (75 x 10cm) rectangle, across the width of the fabric.

Neck tie
From Kim, cut 1: 21½ x 3in (55 x 7.5cm) rectangle, across the width of the fabric.

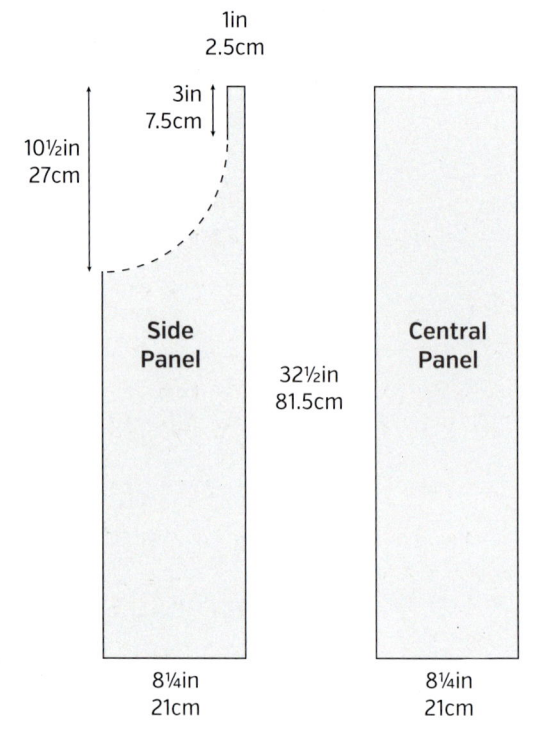

CUTTING GUIDE

Side Panel: 10½in (27cm), 1in (2.5cm), 3in (7.5cm), 32½in (81.5cm), 8¼in (21cm)
Central Panel: 8¼in (21cm)

Apron alternative
You could easily turn this into a skirt apron if the pinafore style is not for you. Use the tab and gathering technique for the top of the bib to create the waist of a skirt apron, running a longer length of narrower ribbon through the tab to create the waist ties.

SEWING THE APRON

Use a ⅝in (1.5cm) seam allowance throughout, unless otherwise stated.

1 With RS facing, pin and stitch the longer edge of the Paperweight side panel to the Ombre central panel. Then repeat to attach the Ombre central panel to the Zig Zag central panel, and finally attach the Zig Zag central panel to the Guinea Flower side panel. To neaten the seams, turn under and edge stitch.

Hemming the armhole edges

2 Turn under ⅝in (1.5cm) along the edge of the armhole, then fold the raw edge under again to meet the crease of the fold. Pin and stitch (**A**). Repeat on the other armhole.

Neck tie

3 Fold the neck tie in half, WS together, and press. Open out and fold the raw edges to the center crease and press flat. Topstitch close to the folded edge along the length (**B**).

4 Check the length of the neck tie and adjust to fit as necessary. Pin to the top RS edge of the apron, with raw edges aligned and the neck tie facing down (**C**). Pin and stitch close to the edge, taking care not to twist the tie.

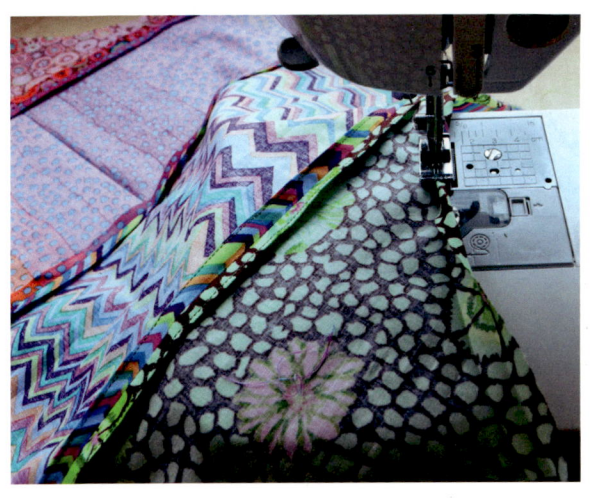

A. Stitching the hem on the armhole.

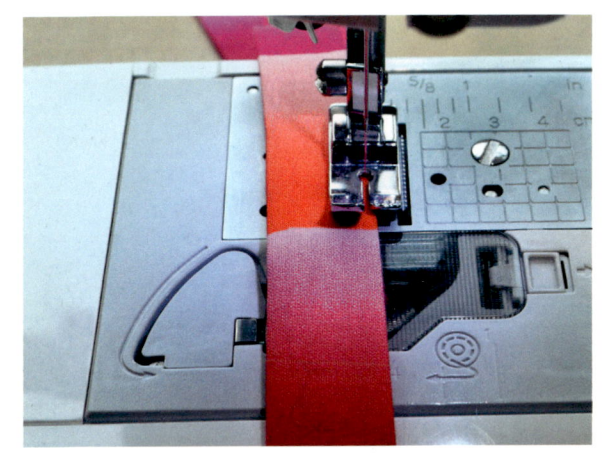

B. Topstitching the folded edge on the tie.

C. Pinning the tie in place.

JAZZ APRON 113

Top casing

5 Turn under ¾in (2cm) along the top edge and crease the fold. Turn under the raw edge by ¼in (6mm). The neck tie should be lying on the WS of the apron. Pin and topstitch across the bottom of the casing (**D**). Make sure that you reverse stitch either end of the seam.

6 Using a bodkin or small safety pin, thread the cotton tape through the casing. Pin at both ends and then gather the casing along the tape to a width of 8in (20cm) (**E**).

7 Fold the ends of the tape under by ½in (1.5cm) and tuck into the casing. Pin securely. With the neck tie facing upward, stitch a small rectangle over the tie and tape. Start stitching on the side to secure the cotton tape, then stitch along the casing seam, up toward the neck tie, and back across the top (**F**). Stitch down the side and reverse stitch to finish.

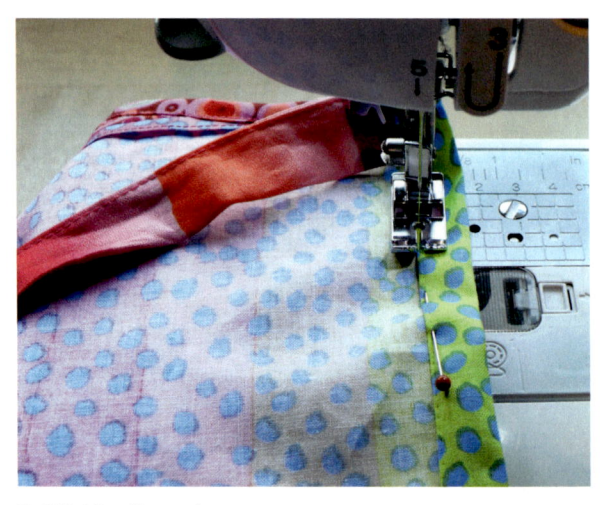

D. Stitching the casing.

E. Gathering the casing.

F. Stitching the tie in place.

Adjustable bib top

If you prefer to have an adjustable top to the bib of the apron, use a longer piece of ribbon cut into two equal lengths so that it can tie at the back neck like the Leafy Apron on page 8.

G. Pinning the waistband in place.

H. Stitching the hem.

FINISHING THE APRON
Adding the waistband
8 Fold the two long edges of the waistband in to meet at the center and press. Position the waistband aligned with the top of the side edges. Pin (G) and topstitch in place on both edges.

Finishing the hem
9 Fold the bottom hem under by ⅝in (1.5cm) and then both sides edges, to achieve a neat edge. Press and edge stitch in place (H).

Attaching the waist ties
10 Fold the long edges of the waist ties in by ⅝in (1.5cm) and press the folds. Fold the tie in half with WS together and press.

11 With RS facing, place the center crease of the waist tie to the top of the side edge of the apron. Pin in place. Take the waist tie over the top of the side edge so the RS of the tie is WS to the apron. Pin and stitch in place (I).

12 Turn the tie out to the right side and edge stitch the join (J). Repeat on the other side.

13 To finish the ends of the waist ties, open out the strip and miter the two corners as shown (K). Re-fold the sides together. Pin and topstitch along the lower edge and the short ends.

I. Pinning the waist tie to the side edge.

J. Edge stitching the tie to the side.

K. Mitering the end of the tie.

JAZZ APRON 115

Patchwork basics

PREPARATION
Work on a good work surface, large enough for your needs, and assemble any materials and equipment before you start. Apart from the usual sewing equipment, a rotary cutter can be useful for accurately cutting long border strips.

If you are making larger patched items, pre-wash all new fabrics before you begin, to ensure that there will be no uneven shrinkage and no bleeding of colors when the finished piece is laundered. Press the fabric whilst it is still damp to return crispness to it.

All fabric requirements in this book are calculated on a 40in (101.5cm) usable fabric width, to allow for shrinkage and selvedge removal.

CUTTING FABRIC
Each project has a number of different elements to cut, so make sure you assemble any templates needed. To make the most efficient use of your fabric, always mark and cut out any border and binding strips first, followed by the largest patch shapes, and finally the smallest ones. The border and binding strips are best cut using a rotary cutter.

Fussy cutting
You can cut out isolated motifs or stripes from printed fabric to make them into a feature in a patchwork block or to create special effects. This is known as "fussy" cutting. Either place your transparent template over the chosen motif on the right side of the fabric, draw around it, and cut out, or cut a window in the template so that you can position the template with greater accuracy.

Cutting angled strips
Some projects require cutting strips of fabric with bias cut ends, cut at 45 degrees. These angled ends will help you to miter corners and join angled strips. To cut at 45 degrees, position a quilter's ruler at the end of the strip and trim away the fabric with a rotary cutter, using the line on the ruler as a guide. Repeat at the other end of the strip, ensuring that your angles are accurate.

MAKING TEMPLATES
Transparent template plastic is the best material to use: it is durable and allows you to see the fabric and select certain motifs, but you can also use thin stiff cardboard or paper (if making hexagons, see page 16).

Templates for machine piecing
1 Trace off the actual-sized template provided either directly onto template plastic, or tracing paper, and then onto thin cardboard. Use a ruler to help you trace off the straight cutting line and any seam lines.
2 Cut out the traced off template using a craft knife, a ruler, and a self-healing cutting mat.
3 Punch holes in the corners of the template, at each point on the seam line, using a hole punch.

Cutting out templates
1 Place the template face down, on the wrong side of the fabric, with the grain line arrow following the straight grain of the fabric, if indicated.
2 Hold the template firmly in place and draw around it with a sharp pencil or fabric marker, marking in any corner dots or seam lines. To save fabric, position patches close together or even touching. Don't worry if outlines positioned on the straight grain when drawn on striped fabrics do not always match the stripes when cut—this will add a degree of visual excitement to the patchwork!
3 Once you've drawn all the pieces needed, you are ready to cut the fabric, with either a rotary cutter and ruler or a pair of sharp sewing scissors.

BASIC MACHINE PIECING
Follow the instructions for the order in which to piece the individual patchwork blocks and then assemble the blocks together in rows.

Sewing blocks (joining squares, strips)

1 Stitch ¼in (6mm) seams using the machine needle plate, a ¼in (6mm) wide machine foot, or tape stuck to the machine as a guide. Pin two patches with right sides together, matching edges.
2 Press the seams of each patchwork block to one side before attempting to join it to another block.
3 When joining rows of blocks, make sure that adjacent seam allowances are pressed in opposite directions to reduce bulk and make matching easier. Pin pieces together directly through the stitch line and to the right and left of the seam. Remove pins as you sew. Continue pressing seams to one side as you work.

Sewing crossed seams

Where four blocks are joined together, you need to take care to match the seams when stitching.

To match intersecting seams, place the RS together and align the seams. Place a pin into the seam of the top fabric, ⅝in (1.5cm) away from the new seam line. Then push the pin into the second seam line, lift the top fabric to check that you are right on the seam line, and then pin through the seams to bring the pin back to the top layer.

To ensure that the seam allowance stays flat under the fabric when sewing the seam, place a pin along the seam allowance, parallel to your new seam.

When you are sewing your crossed seam, sew slowly near to the pin through the seam, leave the needle in the fabric as close to the pin as you can. Remove the pin carefully and the crossed seam will stay in place.

BASIC HAND PIECING

1 Pin two patches with right sides together, so that the marked seam lines are facing outward.
2 Using a single strand of strong thread, secure the corner of a seam line with a couple of back stitches.
3 Sew running stitches along the marked line, working 8–10 stitches per inch (2.5cm) and ending at the opposite seam line corner with a few back stitches. When hand piecing never stitch over the seam allowances.
4 Press the seams to one side, as described in machine piecing (Step 2).

Paper piecing

1 Carefully pin the paper template to the center of the fabric piece. Fold one edge of the shape over the paper, along the seam allowance, and finger press it firmly, using your thumbnail along the fabric on a hard surface.
2 To hold the fold in place, make a couple of basting stitches through the fabric and paper, taking the needle back just before the corner.
3 Fold over the adjacent edge and finger press it as before, making sure the corner is sharp. Continue to baste the folded edge in place.
4 Continue folding, pressing, and basting the fabric over each side of the template. Take care not to pull the basting stitches too tightly or you may distort the shape.
5 Take the first two shapes and place them with the right sides facing. With a short, fine needle and matching thread, place the needle under the fabric turning, bringing the needle out at the corner of the first shape, right on the folded edge.
6 Secure the thread with couple of small stitches and begin to oversew the edges together with small even stitches, just taking in the folded edge.
7 Finally, remove the basting stitches and paper templates when all the pieces are sewn together.

STITCHING TECHNIQUES

Basting
This stitch holds two or more layers of fabric together by sewing by hand or machine with long running stitches. Use a contrasting color thread and start the line of stitching with a few overstitches. Remove basting threads after final stitching.

Ladder stitch
Finger press the seam allowances. Bring the needle up through the fold on one side then take it straight across the gap and insert it into the fold. Make a small stitch through the folded edge and bring the needle out on the edge. Take the the needle back across to the opposite edge and repeat, continuing to zig zag from one side to another and spacing the stitches evenly.

Slip stitching
Used to close gaps in seams. Bring the needle up through the edge of one side of fabric at the start of the gap. Take it across to the opposite side and take a small stitch, pull the thread to close the gap, then take the needle back to the other side and make another small stitch. Continue until gap is closed.

Stitch in the ditch
This is a quilting stitch that follows the seam line and is worked from the front of the work. It is used to quilt and hold the layers of fabric together.

Topstitching and edge stitching
This is a decorative, finishing straight stitch worked on the front of the fabric close to the seam or along an edge but it also useful to prevent fraying on seams.

SPECIAL SEWING TECHNIQUES

Turning a corner
1 When you get to within ½in (12mm) of the corner, reduce the stitch length. At the corners, lower the needle into the fabric, raise the presser foot, and pivot your work.
2 Continue for ½in (12mm) with the reduced stitch length, then return to your normal stitch length (this helps to prevent the fabric from fraying when you trim the corners, prior to turning through to the right side).

Stitching openings
1 When you reach the opening, reverse stitch to fasten the thread and then increase your stitch length to 5 and stitch across the opening.
2 Trim away the corners to reduce the bulk and finger press the seam open all the way round, including where the opening will be.
3 Remove the large stitches across the opening and turn the piece through to the right side. Pull out the corners, you can carefully use a large wooden knitting needle for this job, or tease out with a pin from the right side.
4 Slip stitch or ladder stitch the opening closed. Press.

Adding borders
There are various ways to add borders. You can add straight pieces with square ends (either stitched around the block or stitching two short ends first and then two long ones) or you can create mitered corners (with a 45-degree angle join).

STRAIGHT BORDERS (METHOD 1)
You need to leave enough fabric when you start for the last border piece.
1 Place the edge of the central patchwork, 1¾in (4.5mm) in from the short edge of the border. Begin stitching ¼in (6mm) from the corner of the piece. Press seam to the side.
2 Place the next and following border strips at the edge of the previous border and sew in place. The final border will end level with the edge of the piece.
3 To complete the border, sew the beginning of the first border to the short end of the last.

STRAIGHT BORDERS (METHOD 2)
1 Add the borders to each short end, press seams toward the border.
2 Add the borders to the long ends and press seams toward the border.

MITERED BORDERS (METHOD 3)

First, trim off the ends of the border strips at a 45-degree angle.

1 With the wrong side of center panel facing up, mark each corner, ¼in (6mm) in from each side. Pin from the center of each strip toward the corners. Pin the side borders in position and then stitch from one corner dot to the next, beginning and ending ¼in (6mm) in from the corners of the quilt central panel.

2 Attach the top and bottom border in the same way, stitching from dot to dot.

3 To join the corner seams on the borders, fold the center panel diagonally at a 45-degree angle, from corner to corner. Match the raw edges of the border, pin, and stitch from the dot to the corner of the border. Press the seams open. Fold the panel diagonally in the opposite direction and repeat to sew the two remaining corners.

4 Trim away excess fabric. Attach additional borders in the same way, again beginning from the center of each strip and working toward the corners.

Adding bindings

MAKING BINDING STRIPS

1 Cut bias or straight grain strips the width required for your binding, making sure the grain line is running the correct way on your straight grain strips. Cut enough strips until you have the required length to go around the edge of your quilt or patchwork piece.

2 To join strips together, the two ends that are to be joined must be cut at a 45-degree angle, as above. Stitch right sides together, trim turnings, and press seam open.

3 Fold and press ¼in (6mm) to the wrong side on both long edges of the binding. Then press the binding strip in half lengthwise. Open out the folds. Alternatively, pass binding through a bias binding maker or fold in half and press, then fold the raw edges in to the fold and press once more.

BINDING EDGES

1 With RS facing, pin the bias strip to the edge of the piece, ensuring the raw edges are aligned. Stitch along the fold line of the binding.

2 Fold the binding over to the back of the piece, press along the fold line, pin, and topstitch in place.

BINDING EDGES WITH MITRED CORNERS

1 Cut the starting end of the binding strip at a 45-degree angle, fold a ¼in (6mm) turning to the wrong side along the cut edge and press in place. With wrong sides together, fold the strip in half lengthwise, keeping the raw edges level, and press.

2 Starting at the center of one of the long edges, place the doubled binding onto the right side of the piece, keeping raw edges level. Stitch the binding in place starting ¼in (6mm) in from the diagonal folded edge. Reverse stitch to secure, and work ¼in (6mm) in from edge of the piece toward the first corner. Stop ¼in (6mm) in from corner and work a few reverse stitches.

3 Fold the loose end of the binding up, making a 45-degree angle. Keeping the diagonal fold in place, fold the binding back down, aligning the raw edges with the next side of the piece. Starting at the point where the last stitch ended, stitch down the next side.

4 Continue to stitch the binding in place around all the quilt edges in this way, tucking the finishing end of the binding inside the diagonal starting section.

5 Turn the folded edge of the binding to the back. Slip stitch the folded edge in place just covering binding machine stitches, and folding a miter at each corner.

Piped edges

A piped edge is a decorative finish in which a cord is enclosed in the binding fabric. First you need cut the strips of binding (see left) before you insert the cord.

1 Make the strips of binding, joined if necessary, to match the length of cord to be covered. Press open any seams and lay the piping cord on the wrong side.

2 Wrap the piping cord in the fabric and pin close to the cord, with the pins pointing toward the direction you will be stitching from.

3 Using an adjustable zipper foot, stitch close to but not tight to the piping cord, removing pins as you reach them.

Self-cover buttons

1 Using a self-cover button kit and following the instructions for the size button you are making, cut a scrap of fabric approximately ⅜in (1cm) larger than the button diameter.
2 Place the button on top of the fabric and catch the edge of the fabric under the teeth of the button. When there are no creases around the edge, insert the back of the button with the flange uppermost and press hard, or follow the instructions with your kit.

MAKING CUSHION BACKS

There are various ways to create cushion backs, but the two methods in this book allow you to take the cushion pad out easily. One of them is very simple (the envelope back) consisting of two pieces of overlapping fabric. The other is a back that closes with buttons and buttonholes.

Envelope back

Cut two pieces from your backing fabric, each measuring the width of your cushion and about three-quarters of the length, plus seam allowances.

1 To make a double hem, on the long side of one piece of backing fabric, fold over the raw edge by 1¼in (3cm) to the wrong side, press, then fold over again by 1¼in (3cm) and press again. Machine stitch in place, ¼in (6mm) in from the fold. Repeat on the second piece.
2 Lay the cushion front right side up on your work surface. Position one piece of cushion back wrong side uppermost, aligning raw edges of back and front pieces. Place the second cushion back, wrong side uppermost, so that it is overlapping the first (the righ side of the folded edge of each cushion back piece face inward). Pin the edges in place.
3 Machine sew around all four sides, using a ⅝in (1.5cm) seam. Trim the corners and turn the cushion cover right side out through the envelope fold.

Buttoned cushion back

Cut two rectangles of backing fabric, both the same size, with the long edges measuring the width of the cushion front (including seam allowances), and the short edges measuring half the width plus an extra 3in (7.5cm) for the opening hem and overlaps. Fold over one long raw edge to make a double hem (see Step 1, above).

1 Place the cushion front down, right side facing up.
2 Put one half of the cushion back on top, right side down, with hemmed edge in the center. Place the second back section on the right-hand side, with the hemmed edge in the center. The central 1¼in (3cm) welts should overlap each other exactly.
3 Pin and stitch all the way around. Trim the corners to remove the bulk, neaten the raw edges and turn through to the right side.
4 Mark the position of the buttonholes, spacing them evenly. Then machine stitch each buttonhole in matching threads using a buttonhole foot and cut the buttonholes carefully. Press.
5 Mark the position of the buttons through the center of each buttonhole and sew in place.

BASTING QUILT LAYERS

The quilt top, batting, and backing fabric that make up a quilt need to be held together securely so they don't shift around when you quilt the layers together.

1 Ensure your backing fabric and batting are larger than your quilt top all around—2in (5cm) is usually enough.
2 Place the backing fabric right side down on a smooth, flat surface. Lay the batting on top, aligning the pieces carefully. Next, place your quilt top in the center of the backing and batting, so that you have roughly the same amount of excess batting showing all around. Smooth the quilt with your hands, from the center outward.
3 Take a needle threaded with a long basting thread in a contrasting color to the quilt top and push it into the center of the quilt, through all three layers, and out again. You may find a curved needle is useful for this.
4 Pull the thread through, leaving a small tail but don't knot the thread. Continue stitching long stitches in a spiral shape out toward the edges, ensuring the layers stay smooth and you don't pull too tightly.
5 Once your basting spiral reaches the edges, add further basting stitches to the corners and you are ready to quilt.

121

Templates

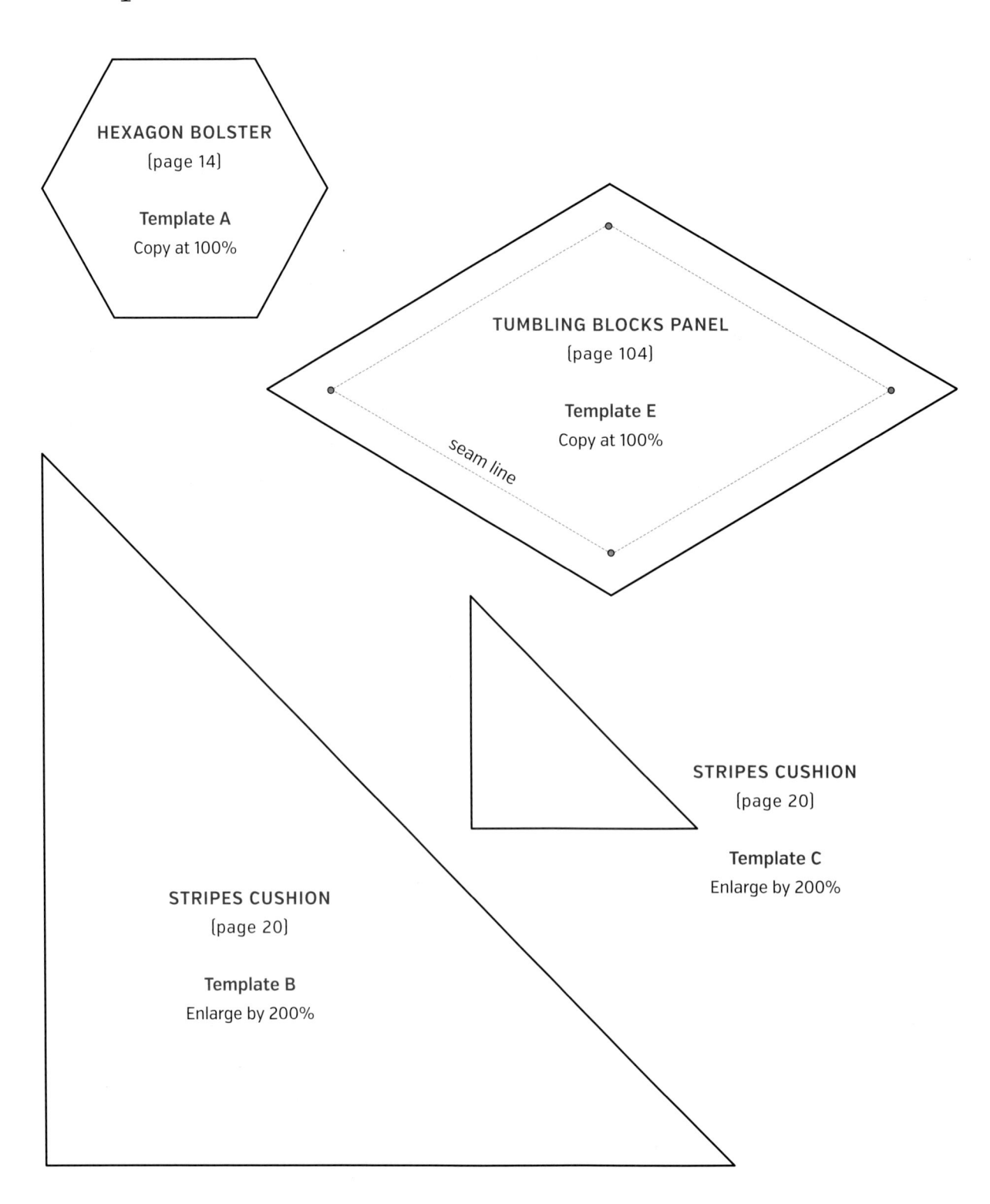

HEXAGON BOLSTER
(page 14)

Template A
Copy at 100%

TUMBLING BLOCKS PANEL
(page 104)

Template E
Copy at 100%

seam line

STRIPES CUSHION
(page 20)

Template C
Enlarge by 200%

STRIPES CUSHION
(page 20)

Template B
Enlarge by 200%

122 KAFFE FASSETT'S BRILLIANT LITTLE PATCHWORKS

BIG TEA COZY
[page 92]

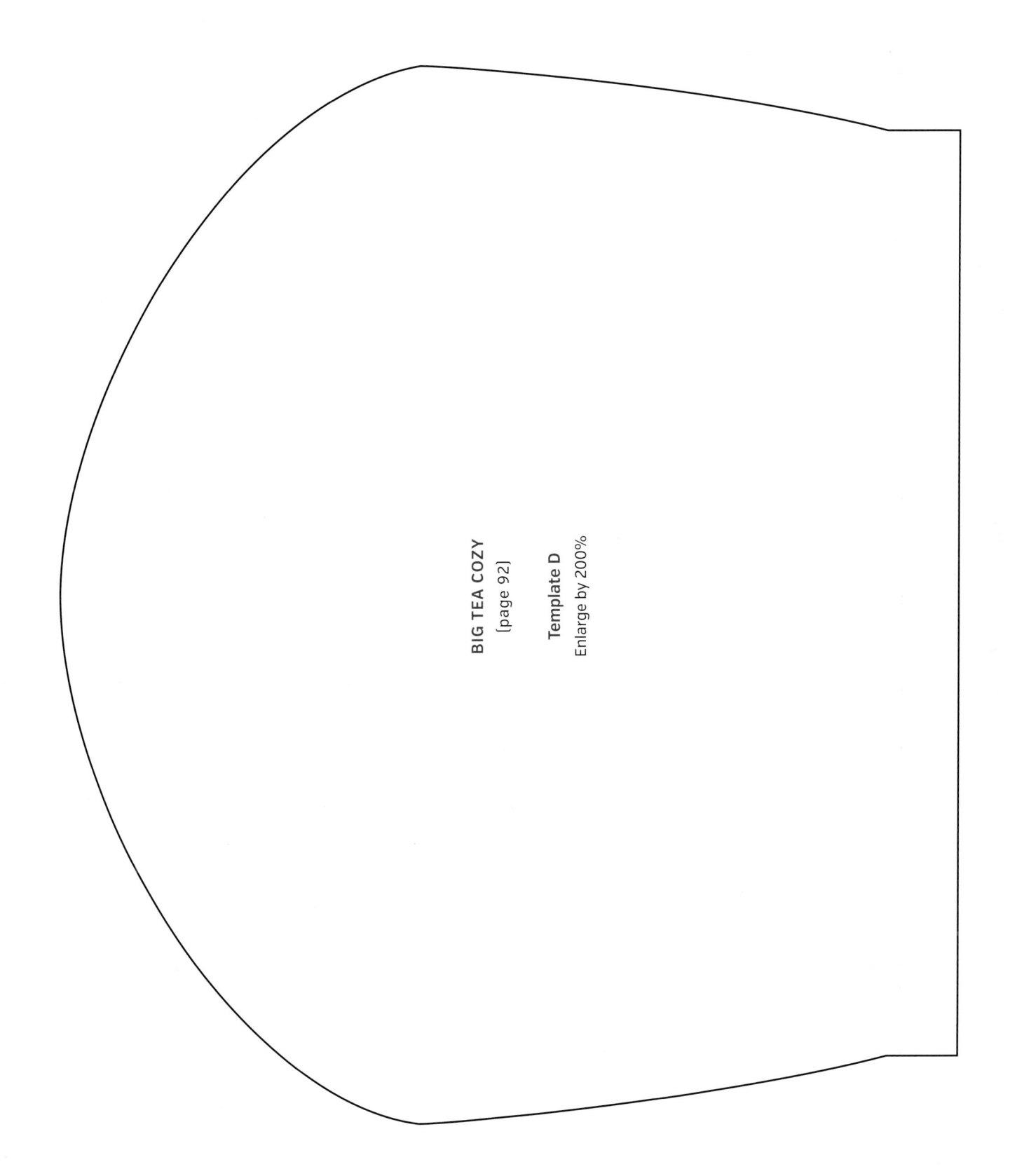

Template D
Enlarge by 200%

Fabrics

Here are the fabric quantities and order codes, and the ribbon sizes and quantities, for each project.

LEAFY APRON (page 8)

Lotus Leaf Antique (GP29)	⅞yd (80cm)
Zig Zag Cool (PWBM043)	¾yd (70cm)
Ribbon: Roman Stripes Blue & Pink 65mm	¾yd (70cm)

HEXAGON BOLSTER (page 14)

Guinea Flower White (GP59)	½yd (45cm)
Guinea Flower Blue (GP59)	¼yd (25cm)
Guinea Flower Pink (GP59)	¼yd (25cm)
Millefiore Blue (GP92)	¼yd (25cm)
Spot China Blue (GP70)	¼yd (25cm)
Spot Red (GP70)	¼yd (25cm)
Paperweight Pastel (GP20)	¼yd (25cm)
Aboriginal Dot Lilac (GP71)	¼yd (25cm)
Aboriginal Dot Mint (GP71)	¼yd (25cm)

STRIPES CUSHIONS (page 20)

RED VARIATION

Roman Stripe Arizona (WROMANX)	½yd (45cm)
Broad Stripe Bliss (WBROADX)	¼yd (25cm)
Caterpillar Stripe Sunshine (WCATERX)	½yd (45cm)

ORANGE VARIATION

Roman Stripe Blood Orange (WROMANX)	½yd (45cm)
Broad Stripe Watermelon (WBROADX)	¼yd (25cm)
Narrow Stripe Red (WNARROW)	½yd (45cm)

SUMMER FLOWERS TABLECLOTH (page 26)

Guinea Flower Mauve (GP59)	2yd (1.8m)
Big Blooms Duck Egg (GP91)	1¾yd (1.6m)
Millefiore Lilac (GP92)	4¼yd (3.85m)
Millefiore Green (GP92)	¼yd (25cm)
Lake Blossoms Yellow (GP93)	¼yd (25cm)
Brassica Yellow (PWPJ051)	¼yd (25cm)
Brassica Pastel (PWPJ051)	¼yd (25cm)
Mad Plaid Pastel (PWBM037)	¼yd (25cm)
Mad Plaid Mauve (PWBM037)	¼yd (25cm)
Zig Zag Pink (PWBM043)	¼yd (25cm)
Lake Blossoms Pink (GP93)	¼yd (25cm)
Lake Blossoms Green (GP93)	¼yd (25cm)

BRASSICA TABLE RUNNER (page 32)

Brassica Green (PWPJ051)	½yd (45cm)
Guinea Flower Green (GP59)	⅜yd (35cm)
Spot Green (GP70)	¾yd (70cm)

FLOWER POWER KIMONO (page 36)

Spot Black (GP70)	⅝yd (60cm)
Japanese Chrysanthemum Red (PJ41)	1¾yd (1.6m)
Spot Royal (PWGP070)	¼yd (25cm)
Lake Blossoms Black (GP93)	½yd (45cm)
Ribbon: Beach Ball Black 38mm	1½yd (1.3m)

BIG BLOOMS MINIQUILT (page 42)

Guinea Flower Turquoise (GP59)	⅜yd (35cm)
Big Blooms Duck Egg (GP91)	¾yd (70cm)
Millefiore Lilac (GP92)	1¼yd (115cm)
Spot Turquoise (GP70)	¼yd (25cm)
Spot China Duck Egg (GP70)	¼yd (25cm)
Zig Zag Pink (PWBM043)	1¼yd (115cm)

FIESTA FLOOR CUSHION (page 48)

Spot Magenta (GP70)	¼yd (25cm)
Roman Stripe Blood Orange (WROMANX)	½yd (45cm)
Zig Zag Warm (PWBM043)	½yd (45cm)
Guinea Flower Pink (GP59)	¼yd (25cm)
Roman Glass Red (GP01)	¼yd (25cm)
Millefiore Tomato (GP92)	¼yd (25cm)
Brassica Red (PWPJ051)	1yd (90cm)

Ribbons:

Roman Stripe Pink & Blue 22mm	3yd (2.75m)
Guinea Flower Green 22mm	2.5yd (2.3m)
Guinea Flower Plum 22mm	⅞yd (80cm)

BLUES TABLE RUNNER (page 56)
Roman Glass Blue (GP01)	¼yd (25cm)
Spot Sky (GP70)	¼yd (25cm)
Aboriginal Dot Iris (GP71)	¼yd (25cm)
Spot China Blue (GP70)	¼yd (25cm)
Guinea Flower Blue (GP59)	⅜yd (35cm)

BLUES TABLE MATS (page 62)
Roman Glass Blue (GP01)	¼yd (25cm)
Spot China Blue (GP70)	¼yd (25cm)
Aboriginal Dot Iris (GP71)	⅜yd (35cm)
Guinea Flower Blue (GP59)	⅜yd (35cm)

LAKE BLOSSOMS STOLE (page 64)
Lake Blossoms Blue (GP93)	1¾yd (1.6m)
Spot Sapphire (GP70)	1¾yd (1.6m)
Ombre Blue (GP117)	1¾yd (1.6m)
Millefiore Blue (GP92)	1¾yd (1.6m)

CHECKERBOARD TOTE BAG (page 68)
Spot Magenta (GP70)	¼yd (25cm)
Spot Royal (PWGP070)	¼yd (25cm)
Spot Black (GP70)	¼yd (25cm)
Spot Green (GP70)	⅜yd (35cm)
Aboriginal Dot Purple (GP71)	¼yd (25cm)
Paperweight Purple (GP20)	⅝yd (60cm)
Ribbon: Plink Black 38mm	2yd (1.8m)

JAPANESE FLOWER CUSHION (page 76)
Gloxinias Natural (PWPJ071)	⅝yd (60cm)
Labels Black (PWBM045)	½yd (45cm)
Aboriginal Dot Red (GP71)	½yd (45cm)

CUBIST STOOL COVER (page 82)
Millefiore Jade (PWGP092)	½yd (45cm)
Caterpillar Stripe Aqua (WCATERX)	⅜yd (35cm)
Narrow Stripe Spring (WNARROW)	⅞yd (80cm)

GIPSY SHAWL (page 88)
Jupiter Red (PWGP131)	1¼yd (1.15m)
Zig Zag Jade (PWBM043)	½yd (45cm)

BIG TEA COZY (page 92)
Big Blooms Emerald (PWGP091)	½yd (45cm)
Jupiter Malachite (PWGP131)	½yd (45cm)
Zig Zag Jade (PWBM043)	½yd (45cm)

LATTICE CHAIR BACK THROW (page 96)
Lake Blossoms Pink (PWGP093)	¾yd (70cm)
Mad Plaid Candy (PWBM037)	¼yd (25cm)
Spot Lavender (GP70)	½yd (45cm)

CHRYSANTHEMUM PANEL (page 100)
Japanese Chrysanthemum Yellow (PJ41)	1yd (90cm)
Aboriginal Dot Lime (GP71)	⅜yd (35cm)
Roman Glass Pastel (GP01)	⅝yd (60cm)
Aboriginal Dot Cream (GP71)	1⅜yd (1.25m)

TUMBLING BLOCKS PANEL (page 104)
Millefiore Brown (GP92)	⅜yd (35cm)
Aboriginal Dot Chocolate (GP71)	⅝yd (60cm)
Aboriginal Dot Pumpkin (PWGP071)	⅜yd (35cm)
Spot Tobacco (GP70)	⅝yd (60cm)

JAZZ APRON (page 110)
Guinea Flower Green (GP59)	¼yd (25cm)
Zig Zag Multi (PWBM043)	1yd (90cm)
Ombre Pink (GP117)	1yd (90cm)
Paperweight Pink (PWGP020)	¼yd (25cm)
Kim Red (PWGP142)	½yd (50cm)

Suppliers

DISTRIBUTORS OF KAFFE FASSETT FABRICS

U.S.A. & CANADA ONLY
Call Toll Free: 866-907-3305
Global Phone: 800-439-5836
www.freespiritfabric.com
www.rowanfabric.com

Westminster Fibers Inc,
Nashua, NH 03060
Tel: 800-445-9276
www.westminsterfibers.com

AUSTRIA
Coats Harlander Ges.m.b.H.
78199 Braeunlingen
Tel: +00800-26 27-2800
Email: ccethread.contactus@coats.com

BENELUX
Coats N.V/Coats B.V.
c/o Coats GmbH
Belgium
Tel: +32 (0) 800-77892
Netherlands: +31 (0) 800-0226648
Luxembourg: +49 (0) 7644-802 222
Email: sales.coatsninove@coats.com

BULGARIA, GREECE, CYPRUS
Coats Bulgaria EOOD
Tel: +359-2-976-77-72
email: officebg@coats.com

CZECH REPUBLIC
Coats Czecho s.r.o.
Stare Mesto 246 Cz-569 32
Tel: +00420-461-619853
Email: galanterie@coats.com

ESTONIA
Coats Eesti AS
Harjumaa, Eesti
Tel: +372 6306 250
Email: communications@coats.com

FINLAND
Coats Opti Crafts Oy
Huhtimontie 6, 04200 Kerava
Tel: +358-9-274871
Email: communications@coats.com

FRANCE
Coats France
159 Avenue de la Marne
BP 94042, 59704 Marcq en Baroeul cedex
Tel: +33 3 20 10 63 63
Email: france.contactus@coats.com

Milpoint
Zaes du moulin rouge 24120
Terrasson
Tel: +33 553 517 420
Email: contact@milpoint.fr

Coats France Division Arts du Fil
c/o Coats GMbH
Tel: +(0) 810-06-00-020
Email: artsdufil@coats.com

GERMANY
Craft Coats GmbH
79341 Kenzingen
Tel: +49 (0) 7644-802 222
Email: communications@coats.com

HUNGARY, SLOVENIA, CROATIA, NORTH SERBIA
Coats Crafts Hungary Kft.
Tel: +36-12332197

ITALY
Coats Cucirini s.r.i.
Viale Sarca, 223 - 20126
Milan
Tel: +39-02-63-61-51
Email: communications@coats.com

LATVIA
Coats Latvija SIA
1004 Riga
Tel: +371-6762-5031
Email: communications@coats.com

LITHUANIA
Coats Lietuva UAB
09310 Vilnius
Tel: +370-5273-0971
Email: communications@coats.com

POLAND
Coats Polska Sp.
91-214 Lodz
Tel: +48-42-254-0400
Email: communications@coats.com

PORTUGAL
Cia. de Linha Coats & Clark, S.A.
Mafamude 4430 Vila Nova de Gaia
Tel: +00-351-223-770-700
Email: communications@coats.com

RUSSIA
Jota + K Moscow
Tel: 007-499 -504-15-84
www.tkani-lifestyle.ru

SLOVAK REPUBLIC
Coats s.r.o.
Tel: +00421-2-63532314
Email: galanteria@coats.com

SPAIN
Coats Fabra. S.A.U.
08027-Barcelona
Tel: +34-93-290-84-95
Email: communications@coats.com

SWEDEN, NORWAY, DENMARK
Coats Industrial Scandinavia
SE-516 22 Dalsjofors, Sweden
Tel: +46 (0)33 225 300
Email: communications@coats.com

SWITZERLAND
Coats Stroppel AG
5417 Untersiggenthal
Tel: +00800-26272800
Email: coats.stroppel@coats.com

TURKEY
Coats Turkiye Iplik Sanayii A.S.
Beykoz 34810 Istanbul
Tel: +90 216 425 8810
Email: turkey.contactus@coats.com

UNITED KINGDOM
Coats Crafts UK
Tel: +01484-681881
Email: ccuk.sales@coats.com
www.webshop.coats.com

The Cotton Patch
1283-1285 Stratford Road
Hall Green
Birmingham B28 9AJ
Tel: +44 121 702 2840
Email: mailorder@cottonpatch.co.uk
www.cottonpatch.co.uk

OTHER RESOURCES

Ribbons
Renaissance Ribbons
P.O. Box 699
Oregon House, CA 95962
Call to Order Toll Free 1-877-422-6601
Customer Service (530) 692-0842
Email: info@RenaissanceRibbons.com
www.renaissanceribbons.com

Foam
Ritchie Foam and Mattress Co.
214 E. Waterlynn Rd
Mooresville, NC 28117
Tel: (704) 663 2533
Email: ritchiefoam@ritchiefoam.com
www.ritchiefoam.com

ACKNOWLEDGMENTS

The author and publishers would like to thank the following people for the part they played in this book: Margaret Rowan for creating the stitched projects so beautifully and for providing the instructions for them; Anne Wilson for her splendid layouts; Debbie Patterson for her scintillating photography; Brandon Mably for managing the location shoot; Belinda Mably for modeling; Katie Hardwicke and Katy Denny for their editing and checking; Therese Chynoweth for the diagrams; and Steven Wooster for flat-shot photography and photoshop work.